IT'S ALL
GREEK
TO ME

Also by Charlotte Higgins
Latin Love Lessons

IT'S ALL GREEK TO ME

FROM HOMER TO THE HIPPOCRATIC OATH, HOW ANCIENT GREECE HAS SHAPED OUR WORLD

CHARLOTTE HIGGINS

HARPER

An Imprint of HarperCollinsPublishers
www.harpercollins.com

HarperCollins books may be purchased for educational, business, or sales
promotional use. For information, please write: Special Markets Department,
HarperCollins Publishers, 10 East 53rd Street, New York, NY 10022.

Illustrations by Mungo McCosh

First published in Great Britain in 2008 by Short Books.

FIRST U.S. EDITION

Library of Congress Cataloging-in-Publication Data is available upon request.

ISBN: 978-0-06-180400-7

10   11   12   13   14   DIX/RRD   10   9   8   7   6   5   4   3   2   1

for PMH and PJH

Contents

IT'S ALL GREEK TO ME

Introduction

ZEUS ONCE LET fly two eagles from the ends of the world: one from the east and one from the west. They soared high over oceans, mountains, forests, and plains, until they met at the very center of the earth, its *omphalos*, or navel. On this spot, a temple to Apollo was dedicated, the home of the Delphic oracle, where those who wished for insight into their past, present, or future might come to consult the god. The questioner would, after making the appropriate payment and sacrifices, be led into the temple's dark heart. In the gloom, the visitor would more sense than see the Pythia—the laurel-crowned woman who acted as the sacred conduit for the god's communications. In a trance, amid the heady fumes of burning laurel and barley, she would begin her utterances: divinely inspired fragments that the priests would interpret and fashion. But as the inquirer passed under the temple colonnade, before he stepped into the inner sanctum itself, he would have seen some letters carved into the portico: *gnothi seauton*—"know thyself."

This extraordinary challenge to achieve self-knowledge still rings out commandingly. It captures one of the things that is most exciting about ancient Greece: from the writings of its greatest thinkers and authors what stands out is an almost visceral need to question, to probe, to debate, to turn accepted opinion on its head—whether the subject of inquiry is the state of the human heart or the nature of justice.

The intellectual achievements of the ancient Greeks were quite simply extraordinary. They shaped the basic disciplines and genres in which we still organize thought: from poetry to drama, from philosophy to history, from natural history, medicine, and ethnography to political science. We have been inexorably molded by ancient Greece: the way we think about right and wrong, about the nature of beauty, goodness, and knowledge; the way we conceive of what it is to be a mortal being amid the immensity of the universe; the way we talk about the past, and our ambiguous relationship with war; the way we discuss politics and citizenship. The tracks that lead back from our world to the Greeks' are narrow, meandering, sometimes virtually rubbed out or invisible—but they are there. What the Greeks did and said still casts light on what we say and do; by looking at the Greeks we can understand more about ourselves. The Greeks, in short, can help us answer their own challenge of "know thyself."

This book is about turning our minds back to ancient Greece, as a way better to grasp our own world, our own hearts. But it is not a love letter to ancient Greece, which, if one were to back-project modern standards upon it, would be revealed as in many ways an appalling place, lacking what we would call human rights, relying on a vast population of slaves regarded as a lower form of life, and rendering women, with very few exceptions, completely invisible. Percy Bysshe Shelley famously said, "We are all Greeks." I hope not.

It is, rather, a love letter to the act of thinking about ancient Greece. In one sense, it's a bluffer's guide, a primer that will give you a helping hand around Greek democracy, or the Persian Wars, or the Parthenon. But it is also a book of enthusiasms and pleasures. If the mighty roll call of Greek writers—Plato, Herodotus, Aeschylus, Sophocles—can seem daunting or inaccessible, I hope to help you to unlock some of their richness, and discover afresh what makes them so exciting, moving, hilarious, and shocking. Reading the Greeks is a joy that is at risk of slipping quietly out of our grasp if classics continues its drift away from curricula and from the mainstream.

To take one example (the most important example): Homer. There is no more gripping, moving account of mortality, war, and the human emotions than the *Iliad*; no better yarn spun than the *Odyssey*, surely the original novel. One of the many things that is so wonderful about reading Homer is that it is not like looking at stylized figures locked in eternal motionlessness on some classical vase. No: Homer is full of living, breathing characters whose dilemmas, griefs, joys, and losses capture us with their intensity and immediacy. We identify with these vivid people—perhaps because, although nearly 3,000 years separate us from their creation, we in the twenty-first century share some of their individualistic, competitive spirit. Homer is the alpha and omega of this book: we shall begin and end with him, because to read Homer is to enter a world of unparalleled and wonderfully sustaining richness; and because Homer is the beginning of understanding so much else in Greek thought and writing.

At this point, it is worth pausing for a moment to consider what this "ancient Greece" actually is. I have been using the phrase blithely, when at best it is a rough and inaccurate shorthand. The world of "ancient Greece" was certainly not confined geographically to the Greek mainland, nor was it a single entity. There were Greek settlements dotted all around the Mediterranean, from Marseilles in the west, to the coast of Asia Minor in the east. In fact, many of the most glamorous intellectuals of ancient Greece came from the coastline of what is now western Turkey. Nor is "Greece" (in Greek "Hellas") a term that would necessarily have been understood by the subjects of this book. "Hellenes" in Homer (the poems were perhaps, though not certainly, written down in the eighth century

BC) simply describe people from a particular region in Thessaly. By the fifth century BC, "Hellas" was understood as meaning roughly the geographical area of modern Greece; and "Hellene" was used by those claiming Greek ethnicity, living anywhere from Sicily to the Black Sea. But in any case, the Greek world was made up of hundreds of politically independent, often disputatious city-states, each with separate systems of government, locally distinct religious cults, even different calendars and names for the months of the year. By the time the historian Herodotus was writing, probably in the third quarter of the fifth century, he could describe Hellenes as united by shared customs, religion, and language. But this notion of "Greekness" was a new idea, a sense of common identity engendered in the wake of the Persian Wars and fostered by the imperial ambitions of the Athenians, in whose interests it was to proclaim an (Athenian-flavored) Greek unity. And in any case, there were plenty of divergences in custom, religion, and language among the Hellenes (there were three main dialects of Greek spoken, with many local variations) even when Herodotus was writing.

It is useful to bear in mind that when we think of "ancient Greece" we tend to be drawn to just one of these hundreds of city-states, and at one particular time: Athens in the fifth century BC. This is perfectly understandable, as during its flowering of power between the routing of the Persians in 479 and its own crushing by Sparta in 404, it was a magnet for writers, artists, and thinkers from all over the Greek world, and the scene of the most exciting intellectual revolution that the world has ever witnessed. The Athenians have always made the most noise; and they left us an abundance of literary masterpieces, not least the great dramas of Aeschylus, Sophocles, and Euripides, written for performance at the Athenian festival called the City Dionysia. Still, it is worth remembering that the Athenians weren't the only Greeks, nor were they even "representative" Greeks. It's also worth pointing out that, because this book has to stop somewhere, I have confined its scope to the period spanned by the works of Homer and Hesiod at the earliest (eighth century BC), and Aristotle (fourth century BC) at the latest, though influential literature was still produced and great scientific discoveries still made by Greeks after Philip of Macedon and his son Alexander the Great had brought Greece, and most of the rest of the known world, into their empire in the late fourth century.

To resume, then: it is worth thinking about ancient Greece because it brings us a perspective on the way we live now, from our politics to our sense of history. And reading the Greeks is also a source of unbounded enrichment and pleasure. But even more important than all this, perhaps, is the idea of "ancient Greece" not simply as a specific place or a time, but a realm where the imagination, the emotions, and the intellect can roam free. Thinking about the ancient Greeks is always provisional. We will never completely grasp ancient Greece. An enormous wealth of literature, art, architecture, and other artifacts have survived, but for every survival, there are a thousand losses. We have twenty dramas by Euripides, but we know that his complete works numbered ninety plays. For Aeschylus, we have seven extant out of ninety. And for Sophocles, just seven out of 123. Works that were seen as masterpieces in antiquity are nothing but dust, ashes, and the occasional quote in other texts: take, for example, Ephorus of Cyme's thirty-volume history of the known world from the eleventh century to 340—famous in antiquity, now gone, and never to be recovered. (Unless the generous sands of Egypt, which have turned up many well-preserved papyri, produce another miracle.)

Virginia Woolf put our distance from the Greeks beautifully in her essay "On Not Knowing Greek." She said that we are separated from them by "a chasm which the vast tides of European chatter can never succeed in crossing"; as opposed to our experience of, say, Chaucer: "We are floated up to him insensibly on the current of our ancestors' lives." But these gaps, these lacunae, that distance, allow each generation and each individual to create his or her own ancient Greece—a partial, fragmentary ancient Greece onto which our own desires and preoccupations can be released and our intellects let loose to play. "Back and back we are drawn to steep ourselves in what, perhaps, is only an image of the reality, not the reality itself, a summer's day imagined in the heart of a northern winter," wrote Woolf.

For me, the writing of Plato is a wonderful metaphor for our relationship with ancient Greece. Plato did not write in the form of treatises; he did not propound theories, even—or at least not in a straightforwardly doctrinaire way. Plato's philosophy is almost always written as dialogues between two or more speakers: its very form encapsulates disagreement, debate, and provisional answers rather than unshakeable dogma. Incompleteness, as it were, is at its heart. In the same way, knowledge of ancient Greece is fugitive, fragile, difficult to grasp. When the mind travels to ancient Greece, it embarks on a quest: an idea C. P. Cavafy, the great modern Greek poet, put beautifully in his poem "Ithaca," which takes the idea of Odysseus' homecoming:

> When you set out for distant Ithaca,
> fervently wish your journey may be long,—
> full of adventures and with much to learn.
>
> Translation: J. C. Cavafy

And, as we set out on that long but rewarding journey toward Ithaca, we will come closer to answering that ancient challenge: *gnothi seauton*.

Note on names and dates: *names are rendered in their familiar Latinized versions rather than transliterated from Greek. Dates are all BC, except where stated.*

1. The alpha and the omega:
Why a life without Homer is a life half-lived

"On First Looking Into Chapman's Homer"

Much have I travelled in the realms of gold
And many goodly states and kingdoms seen;
Round many western islands have I been
Which bards in fealty to Apollo hold.
Oft of one wide expanse had I been told
That deep-browed Homer ruled as his desmesne;
Yet did I never breathe its pure serene
Till I heard Chapman speak out loud and bold:
Then felt I like some watcher of the skies
When a new planet swims into his ken;
Or like stout Cortez when with eagle eyes
He stared at the Pacific—and all his men
Looked at each other with a wild surmise—
Silent, upon a peak in Darien.

John Keats

ONE NIGHT IN October 1816, Charles Cowden Clarke showed his old schoolfriend John Keats translations of the *Iliad* and the *Odyssey* by George Chapman—the first versions in English of Homer's epic poems, published in 1611 and 1615 respectively. Keats, whose Greek was very patchy, knew Homer via translations by John Dryden and Alexander Pope, but Chapman's earthy, vigorous, yompingly pacey verse was a world away from Pope's neatly polished, rather mincing heroic couplets. The two friends plunged into the book, reading it together, unable to drag themselves away till dawn: it was an experience of "teeming wonderment," Cowden Clarke remembered. At ten o'clock that morning, as he came downstairs after snatching a few hours' sleep, Cowden Clarke found an envelope on his breakfast table. Inside was a sheet of paper, and on it was scrawled Keats's famous sonnet, "On First Looking Into Chapman's Homer."

In the almost 3,000 years since the *Iliad* and the *Odyssey* were composed, readers have been responding to these poems just as Keats did: with the excitement, awe, and sense of revelation "some watcher of the skies" might feel when "a new planet swims into his ken."

If you haven't read them, you have an enriching experience in store: you will be handed the key to a world of incredible storytelling, and profoundly beautiful poetry. The great writers of today, of course, are still learning from Homer: Philip Pullman, author of the *His Dark Materials* trilogy, and former schoolteacher, says this: "I was allowed to tell the *Iliad* and the *Odyssey* to my classes simply because I thought it would be a good idea, and I told both those stories to three classes each year for twelve years. I learned more about storytelling from that than from anything else; I mean about how to time the cliffhangers, how to slow down and speed up, exactly how much detail you need to give in order to let them see the scene in their minds. And it was vital to tell them in my own words rather than read out someone else's version."

Furthermore, the world of Homer is also a world in which the big questions are explored, with extraordinary humanity and compassion: the appalling tragedy of dying young; the effects of war; how one can feel pity and empathy toward one's greatest enemies; what is heroism; what it means to grow up; what is the nature of true love and marriage; what is a home. Homer is a rip-roaring read, he makes you laugh and he makes you weep like a child. Homer's poems are (probably) the earliest surviving works of European literature: and they remain, to many people's minds, the greatest. You just can't do without them.

The poems are also the starting point for getting to grips with the Greeks. That's because the Greeks were, quite understandably, obsessed with the *Iliad* and the *Odyssey*. This is how the writer Heraclitus described the place of Homer in the first century AD:

> From the very earliest infancy young children are nursed in their learning by Homer, and swaddled in his verses we water our souls with them as though they were nourishing milk. He stands beside each one of us as we set out and gradually grow into men, he blossoms as we die, and until old age we never grow tired of him, for as soon as we set him aside we thirst for him again; it may be said that the same limit is set to both Homer and life.
>
> Translation: Richard Hunter

It's a wonderful image of the place Homer occupied in Greek life—"mother's milk," so to speak. But it's also a testament, which still holds true, to the richness of Homer, to the way that you can read him over and over again and still find something fresh.

And when people talk about Homer's being the fountainhead of European thought, that really is no exaggeration. To a quite startling degree, subsequent Greek writing was a development of, or a reaction to, Homer, and thus—given the extent to which Greek thought is the progenitor of modern Western culture—he still leaves indelible marks on the way we see the world today.

For instance: the Greeks, as far as the Western world is concerned, invented drama (that means without the Greeks, no plays or films). And to a very large degree, the great Greek tragic playwrights—Aeschylus, Sophocles, and Euripides—found their material in Homer. Aeschylus' great trilogy the *Oresteia* is a kind of sequel to events related in Homer; it's a "what happened next" to Agamemnon, the leader of the Greek forces in the *Iliad*. Ditto Euripides' *Trojan Women*: it fleshes out what happens to the female members of the Trojan royal family, all of whom we have met in the *Iliad*, dramatizing the dreadful humiliation of their fate as enslaved captives. Another example is Herodotus, the man who invented the concept of history. When Herodotus writes down the causes and events of a real conflict—in this case, the Persian Wars—he defines what he is doing directly in relation to the *Iliad*. He even records (though rejects) the theory that the causes of the Persian Wars go right back to semi-mythical, tit-for-tat abductions of women between Asia and Europe, including that of Helen of Troy.

If you were giving a compliment to an ancient Greek, the highest praise possible was to compare him or her to Homer. Herodotus was called the prose Homer; the poet Sappho was called the female Homer. "Homer was the epic Sophocles, and Sophocles a tragic Homer," ran an aphorism relating to the great playwright. (About half of the lines in the epics are in direct speech, so you could say that Homer was already halfway to drama.) Even revolutionary thinkers who wanted to challenge the status quo and topple Homer couldn't help dealing with him: Plato couldn't ignore him; he had to at least engage with him as he banished the poet from his putative *Republic*.

So what are these epics all about? The stories of both the *Iliad* and the *Odyssey* are rooted in the Trojan War, a mythical conflict between a band of Greek allies and the Trojans, inhabitants of a city on what is now the Mediterranean coast of Turkey. (I say mythical: the poems probably have their roots in long-ago memories of Greek raids on the Turkish coast, perhaps even a real war between Greeks and Trojans.) The poems are set in the hazy, distant past, when gods and men had free dealings with one another, and when men were stronger and better than they are now.

The war had started because Paris, prince of Troy, was asked to judge a beauty contest between three goddesses, Hera, Athena, and Aphrodite. Each offered him bribes: that of Aphrodite, the winning goddess, was marriage to the most beautiful woman in the world. Unfortunately, to say the least, that woman—Helen—was already married, to Menelaus, king of Sparta. When Paris and Helen disappeared to Troy together, Menelaus and his brother, the powerful Agamemnon, king of Mycenae, assembled an army of allies from all over the mainland and the islands, from Achilles' force of Myrmidons from Phthia, to Nestor's troops from Pylos, to Odysseus' from Ithaca.

The Greeks (or rather, as they are called in Homer, the Achaeans, or Danaans, or Argives, but we'll stick with Greeks for simplicity here) then laid siege to Troy. It was a grueling, ten-year-long business, the deadlock broken only when Odysseus, that expert tactician, hit on the notion of the Wooden Horse. The trick was to pretend that the entire expeditionary force had packed up and sailed west—leaving only a vast wooden horse behind them. The Trojans, despite repeated warning from the unfortunate princess Cassandra (doomed to make accurate prophecies that no one believed), thought the horse was an offering to the god Poseidon, so they dragged it through the city gates. But it was hollow, and contained the Greeks' best warriors—who scrambled out of the horse while the Trojans were throwing their victory party, and torched, looted, and massacred their way through the city.

So much for the backstory. The action of the poem actually takes place during a fraction of that ten-year stretch: it is set over the course of about forty days in the tenth year of the conflict, before the

Wooden Horse was ever thought of. The subject of the poem is announced right away, in its very first word:

> Rage—Goddess, sing the rage of Peleus' son Achilles,
> murderous, doomed . . . *

The rage here is not Greek rage against Trojan, but Greek against Greek. The conflict at the heart of the *Iliad* is between Agamemnon, king of Mycenae and commander-in-chief of the Greek forces, and his best warrior, Achilles. Agamemnon may be in charge—but he's no match for the brilliant and temperamental Achilles, by far the best fighter in the army. What has happened is this: At the beginning of the poem, the Greeks are being afflicted by a plague that is cutting a terrible swathe through the troops. In order to stop it, they learn, Agamemnon must return one of his captive girls to her father, a Trojan priest of Apollo. To avoid losing face, Agamemnon demands that Achilles, in turn, hand over to him one of his captive women. Achilles is furious at the affront, and though he complies, he exacts a grotesque revenge.

For Achilles is not like other men. His mother is a goddess, Thetis; he has unique access to divine power. Thetis persuades Zeus, king of the gods, to carry out Achilles' wishes and turn the tide of war dramatically against the Greeks (though their eventual victory is foreordained). Achilles withdraws from the fighting and sulks

---

* For a book-by-book summary of the *Iliad* and *Odyssey*, see pp. 36–41. The translation used here is not George Chapman's—which begins with the lovely "Achilles' baneful wrath—resound, O goddess"—but Robert Fagles' for Penguin Classics, which was published in 1990 and followed six years later by his *Odyssey*. There are innumerable translations available, but for my money, Fagles' is the one: vivid, and with just the right kind of roughness. It is also brilliant to read out loud. So I am going to use it throughout, and line numbers will refer to his version.

The world of the *Iliad*

in his tent. The bulk of the poem charts the Greeks' increasingly desperate fortunes.

It's not straightforward, however. The battling for Troy is mirrored by a conflict in heaven. The gods have taken sides—Athena, Hera, and Poseidon favouring the Greeks; Apollo, Aphrodite, and Ares, the Trojans. Scheming, clever, and strong, Athena and Hera will do anything they can to subvert Zeus' commands and try to give their favorite Greek heroes an advantage—especially Diomedes, whom they build up so much that (in Book 5) he battles the gods, wounding Aphrodite and even Ares, god of war. But by Book 9 the

Greeks are getting desperate. The Trojan champion Hector, son of King Priam, is slaughtering Greeks and sending terror into their ranks. An embassy of leaders is sent to Achilles' tent to try to get him to relent. Nothing doing.

Finally, however, Achilles softens to the extent that he allows his beloved friend Patroclus into the fray. Patroclus straps on Achilles' armour (this is Book 16) and goes off to fight . . . but he dies, downed by Hector.

Achilles' reaction, when he is told about this disaster in Book 18, is monumental, extreme:

> A black cloud of grief came shrouding over Achilles.
> Both hands clawing the ground for soot and filth,
> he poured it over his head, fouled his handsome face
> and black ashes settled onto his fresh clean war-shirt.
> Overpowered in all his power, sprawled in the dust,
> Achilles lay there, fallen . . .
>
> *Iliad* 18 24–29

When the grief-stricken Achilles finally enters the battle it is a supernatural event. He is a berserker, unstoppable. Book 21 of the poem is a bloodbath: so completely does he choke the river Scamander with Trojan corpses that the river itself is outraged and rises up to fight him. But even the river can't match Achilles, and at last he runs across the plain to the gate of Troy, outside which Hector is waiting.

Shockingly, when he sees Achilles coming, Hector takes to his heels and flees. Achilles pursues him remorselessly, round and round the city. On the fourth lap, finally, they fight, and Hector dies. But Achilles' anger is still unquenched. He takes Hector's body and lashes it onto the back of his chariot, the hero's head dragging in the dust. Even having exacted this gruesome revenge for Patroclus' death, Achilles cannot sleep; he takes solitary walks up and down the beach, every once in a while taking out his chariot and dragging

Hector's body around Patroclus' tomb again. Even by the standards of Homeric heroes (who don't exactly stint, emotionally) the feeling is he has gone too far. One night, Zeus allows Priam, the old king of Troy—Hector's father—to steal into the Greek encampment at night and ransom the body of his son. In one of the most moving scenes in all literature, Priam kneels at Achilles' feet and kisses his hands—the hands that killed his own son—and asks the younger man to remember his own father, old, frail, and far away.

> Those words stirred within Achilles a deep desire
> to grieve for his own father. Taking the old man's hand
> he gently moved him back. And overpowered by memory
> both men gave way to grief. Priam wept freely
> for man-killing Hector, throbbing, crouching
> before Achilles' feet as Achilles wept himself,
> now for his father, now for Patroclus once again,
> and their sobbing rose and fell throughout the house.
>
> *Iliad* 24 592–599

There's so much richness in the *Iliad*—and Homer is going to be a thread that runs right through this book. I just want to mention here one or two of the things that make it so incredibly memorable and striking. First, what's immediately noticeable about the poem is its evenhandedness. The Trojans, despite being officially on the "wrong side," are not demonized, or seen as inferior to the Greeks in any particular way. Hector is a fully formed, flesh-and-blood character with whom we empathize—his death is a traumatic, terrible event. That's partly because of the way Homer sketches in his life beyond the battlefield. We are given an incredibly moving glimpse of Hector as a family man, as a husband who loves his wife and child. We see, in other words, what Hector is fighting for, and precisely what he is going to lose.

That leads directly to my next point, which is, although there is a hell of a lot of fighting in Homer, the battle and bloodshed is very much a backdrop to human conflicts, dramas, and dilemmas: the pity, the heartbreaking cruelty of young men doomed to die; the fascination and enigma of characters such as Achilles, who is both magnificent, emotionally rich, and at the same time grotesquely ruthless. In other ways, too, Homer changes the mood or widens the poem's perspective—through his beautiful poetic imagery (of which more in chapter 5) and often through the gods, whose motivations are an intriguing, sometimes even funny counterpoint to the human drama (more on this in the next chapter).

For now, I will mention just two other points about the brilliance of the *Iliad*. First is the architecture of the poem. The storytelling is very simple. It starts at the beginning and works through to the end. Barring the occasional "meanwhile," this is a linear narrative. But what a stroke of genius it is to absent the main character, Achilles, between Books 2 and 16 (excepting a brief emergence in Book 9 when he receives the embassy). The effect when he passes into full focus, from getting the news of Patroclus' death to his entry into the battle and slaughter of Hector, is shocking, stunning. After books and books of fighting and poignant deaths and great feats of warriordom, you suddenly realize you haven't seen anything like the real thing; that, though gripping, it was like watching something in black-and-white only for the film to suddenly be switched into Technicolor—and with the most extraordinary special effects. Everything becomes a concentrated version of what it was: things get bloodier, more emotional, more anguished. And so when the final encounter occurs between Priam and Achilles (which is very far from a reconciliation; it's an edgy, tense meeting that you feel could go badly wrong at any moment), it is all the more affecting. I defy anyone not to weep at Book 24 of the *Iliad*.

Finally, one other tiny thing. Part of the pleasure of the *Iliad* is its flesh-and-bloodness, its materiality, the fact that you can see and feel the sweat, the bronze, the leather, the sand, the blood. Sometimes I find it hard not to think of cinema when reading it: of a camera going into close-up, or panning out. Two examples. One is when Menelaus is wounded in Book 4. The gush of blood over his haunches, says Homer, is like a piece of ivory, a prized horse's cheekpiece, that has been dyed blood-red by a Carian or Maeonian woman. That close-up gush of red over Menelaus' ivory-white thighs couldn't be more vivid. Second, at the end of Book 8, Homer's eye pans out deep above the Trojan army encampment after nightfall. The campfires, he says, are like the stars:

> Hundreds strong, as stars in the night sky glittering
> round the moon's brilliance blaze in all their glory
> when the air falls to a sudden, windless calm . . .
> all the lookout peaks stand out and the jutting cliffs
> and the steep ravines and down from the high heavens bursts
> the boundless bright air and all the stars shine clear
> and the shepherd's heart exults—so many fires burned
> between the ships and the Xanthus' whirling rapids
> set by the men of Troy, bright against their walls.
>
> *Iliad* 8 640–649

The *Odyssey* is quite a different sort of poem altogether. The *Iliad* is geographically constricted: aside from occasional trips to Mount Olympus, the action is mostly confined to the area between the Greeks' beached ships and the city of Troy. By contrast, the hero of the *Odyssey* gets . . . everywhere. The story, as you'll know, concerns Odysseus, who, after the end of the Trojan War, is endlessly thwarted (having offended the sea god, Poseidon) in his attempts to return to his beloved island of Ithaca. After ten years at Troy, this business of getting home takes another decade, during which he has to survive the Cyclops, the terrifying Scylla and Charybdis, and outmaneuver several wily women. (The nymph Calypso is one:

she holds him against his will on her island, Ogygia, for seven years, hoping he'll marry her. The other is the witch Circe, who, although she turns out to be a good egg in the end, starts off by turning many of Odysseus' shipmates into pigs.)

As in the *Iliad*, the subject of the *Odyssey* is summed up in its first word—man. It is the story of a man, as Robert Fagles translates it "of twists and turns, / driven time and again off course, once he had plundered / the hallowed heights of Troy. / Many cities of men he saw and learned their minds, many pains he suffered, heartsick on the open sea . . ." The poem's tonal range is as wide as its geographical reach. Odysseus, the king, warrior, and strategist of the *Iliad*, lives every kind of life in the *Odyssey*, from honored, kingly guest, to shipwrecked sailor who washes up on a beach without a scrap on him, to beggar—a disguise he adopts to avoid immediate recognition when he comes back to his troubled home turf. If the heroes of the *Iliad* live by the sword, the hero of the *Odyssey* lives by his wits. The range of characters is much broader than in the *Iliad*, too: with a couple of exceptions, the dramatis personae of that poem are kings and gods, with the odd noblewoman thrown in. In the *Odyssey*, by contrast, we have maids, cowherds, swineherds, nymphs, gods, monsters, queens, bards, blushing virginal princesses . . .

We think, perhaps, of the *Odyssey* being about the Cyclops and all that; the hero's rather baroque adventures as he shifts about the Mediterranean. But there are really two strands at play in the *Odyssey*—the hero's travels on the one hand, and on the other, what's going on back home in Ithaca, in particular with his son, Telemachus. (And unlike the *Iliad*, it's not a story told "straight" but with complicated flashbacks and actions happening simultaneously in different locations, a narrative technique entirely appropriate to the story's hero, the man "of twists and turns.") The two threads weave themselves together in the second half of the poem when, in Book 13, Odysseus reaches Ithaca; and the rest of the story concerns the hero's re-establishing himself as the rightful king. That involves plotting a terrible revenge on those who have been disloyal, principally the suitors who have been badgering his wife Penelope to choose a husband from among them. Odysseus turns the banqueting hall of his palace into a charnel house; by the end the dead suitors are piled up like a catch of fish on the beach.

The *Odyssey* begins as the goddess Athena, taking advantage of the temporary absence of Poseidon, decides to help Odysseus return home. Her plan is twofold: to get Odysseus off Ogygia, and out of the clutches of Calypso; and to send his young son Telemachus off on a journey to mainland Greece to see if he can discover any news about his father. Barely meeting Odysseus for the first four books of the poem, we begin with Telemachus and Ithaca.

In those first few books of the *Odyssey*, another story has a habit of cropping up, apparently in passing—that of Agamemnon's return to Argos. After ten years' absence, and his victory over the Trojans, he returned home only to be slaughtered unceremoniously by his wife's lover Aegisthus—who in turn, was murdered by Orestes, Agamemnon's son. It's a sort of alternative storyline . . . if Penelope were disloyal; if Odysseus were daft enough to enter his kingdom covered in pomp and circumstance rather than using his resources of wit and subterfuge—then this is how this story *could* end. And it's also a challenge to Telemachus: Orestes had the guts to avenge his father. Can the boyish Telemachus live up to that example?

An important part of the story of the *Odyssey* is Telemachus' journey to manhood, and his recognition that he is the true son of Odysseus, this man whom he has never seen. At the beginning of the poem, when Athena appears to Telemachus in disguise, he tells her he *thinks* he is Odysseus' son, that's what his mother has always told him, but he really can't be sure. By the end of the poem he has become, truly, his father's son; he has grown up. Part of the point of Athena's sending him off across the seas to question his father's old war comrades is, for sure, to get news of Odysseus. But it's also to discover, from those who really know him, what kind of a man his father is, and how to be the son of that father. The circle, in a way, is completed in Book 24, when Odysseus reveals himself to *his* father, the ancient Laertes: at that moment, the peace and harmony of a household gone dangerously awry is fully put to rights.

There's also, I suppose, a sort of moral satisfaction in the *Odyssey*, almost the feel of a fairy tale. The world is out of joint and it gets put to rights (albeit with a rather grotesque brutality). People, in the end, get to recognize who they are, who their family is, their place in the universe. There's a "do-as-you-would-be-done-by" element: Odysseus is constantly being cast among strangers whose moral worth is judged on how they treat the newcomer, the "guest." Is the host courteous, kind, and generous like Eumaeus, the old swine-herd in Ithaca, who behaves beautifully even though he does not yet recognize this disreputable old beggar as his king? Or is he an uncivilized brute like Polyphemus, the Cyclops, who jokes that his "guest-gift" to Odysseus will be to eat him . . . last (more on this in chapter 6). But the *Odyssey* is also the greatest of adventure stories, a wonderful yarn. T. E. Lawrence, who made a rather bad transla-tion of it, was surely right to call it "the first novel of Europe." And for salty old sea dogs it's a joy: the poem really does almost smell of the ocean.

Finally, a note on one of the most striking aspects of both poems—their incredible poetic imagery. Extended similes are a fa-vorite technique in both poems, and beautiful alternative worlds are created with these images. Armies are like whirlwinds or wildfire; heroes are like mountain lions or hawks going for the kill; young warriors dying are like saplings felled on a riverbank. (There's more on this in chapter 5.) Here's an example: when Achilles is running across the Trojan plain from the river towards the Scaean gate to take on Hector, his breastplate (this is Homer panning out the camera again) flashes like Sirius, the dog star, whose late-summer rising was supposed to bring death and disease . . .

> And old King Priam was first to see him coming,
> surging over the plain, blazing like the star
> that rears at harvest, flaming up in its brilliance—
> far outshining the countless stars in the night sky,
> the star they call Orion's Dog—brightest of all
> but a fatal sign emblazoned on the heavens,
> it brings such killing fever down on wretched men.
> So the bronze flared on his chest as on he raced.
>
> *Iliad* 22 31–38

The imagery in the *Odyssey* is no less vivid but often a little less exalted. There's a hilarious simile where Odysseus can't sleep, and he tosses and turns like a sausage being turned on a grill by a cook. In another, when he's clinging onto a reef during one of his shipwrecks, and a huge wave crashes over him, hurling him out to sea, it is:

> Like pebbles stuck in the suckers of some octopus
> dragged from its lair—so strips of skin torn
> from his clawing hands stuck to the rock face.
>
> *Odyssey* 5 476–478

This image has been used in turn in a lovely little poem by Michael Longley to talk about the way he sees Homer: still full of riches:

> . . . like Homer's octopus
> Yanked out of its hidey-hole, suckers
> Full of tiny stones, except that the stones
> Are precious stones or semi-precious stones.

Longley's lines also remind me of C. P. Cavafy's poem "Ithaca," which I quoted in the introduction to this book, and which talks about the *Odyssey* as a journey through life, as a quest for knowledge. Here is another part of it:

> Fervently wish your journey may be long.
> May they be numerous—the summer mornings
> when, pleased and joyous, you will be anchoring
> in harbours you have never seen before.
> Stay at the populous Phoenician marts,
> and make provision of good merchandise;
> coral and mother of pearl; and ebony
> and amber; and voluptuous perfumes
> of every kind, in lavish quantity.
> Sojourn in many a city of the Nile,
> and from the learned learn and learn amain.
>
> Translation: J. C. Cavafy

May you too enjoy your journey through Homer: the joy of it is that the riches that come from the *Iliad* and the *Odyssey*—the precious and semi-precious stones, the mother-of-pearl, the coral, the amber, the ebony—come from a store that is inexhaustible.

THE HOMERIC QUESTION

One thing that you'll notice if you read any Homer is a habit of repeated phrases to describe particular things or people. The sea is wine-dark; the dawn is rosy-fingered, Athena is gray-eyed. There are innumerable other examples, some of them unique to particular characters, some less specific. You'll also find that certain scenes are repeated, or come with only minor variations: for instance, sacrifices and meals are often described in a similar way, as are episodes where heroes put on their armor.

What's this all about? Well, this rather neatly gets us into what's known as the Homeric Question, which is one of those big, knotty problems that has driven scholars crazy for centuries. The Homeric Question is, in fact, a cluster of questions about how the epic poems were composed, and how and when and why and by whom they were written down.

In antiquity commentators seemed united in agreeing that both poems were by a poet called Homer, but in the late-eighteenth century this view was challenged by the so-called "analysts," who recognized that the roots of the poems went way back before the adoption of writing by the Greeks, and drew on an oral tradition of bardic song. Analysts proposed that the *Iliad* and the *Odyssey* were in effect a patchwork of contributions from different bards. Some parts of the poems were seen to be inferior; there was a theory that, with sufficiently robust scholarship, you would be able to extract a sort of ur-*Iliad* purified of these accretions.

A major moment in the history of the question came in the 1920s and '30s when the scholar Milman Parry and his student Albert Lord traveled to Yugoslavia and studied the methods of the *guslars*, the oral epic poets there. (You can get a wonderful fictionalized flavor of what this might have been like by reading Ismael Kadaré's book *The File on H*, a story of two scholars researching Albanian oral poetry.) Parry and Lord's study of the methods of modern oral bards made them realize that the repeated phrases and episodes must have been memory-aids for the bards.

The point is that the Homeric epics are composed in a verse form that is based on the number and length of syllables in a given line (rather than stressed syllables like most English verse). So having a phrase like "much-enduring Odysseus," prefabricated, as it were, in the correct meter, would be very useful to someone relying on memory and improvisation. Ditto your rosy-fingered dawn and wine-dark sea. Meanwhile, whole repeated scenes could become a sort of framework for the poet, to be dressed up with variations and distinctive details depending on the context.

That work was incredibly important, but it didn't settle the Homeric Question; in fact, there is still no real consensus. Some people believe the *Iliad* and the *Odyssey* are so different they must be by different people. Some people have questioned the very notion of "authorship": since the poems are the fruits of a long tradition of oral poetry handed down from bard to bard, they argue that the poems are the result of a centuries-long process quite different from the "event" of individual creation that we think of when talking about a novel by Austen or Dickens. Some people, at the opposite extreme, have thought that the poems are so beautifully constructed, with such delicately balanced architecture, they can't possibly have been "just" sung, but must have been composed with the help of literary tools and techniques.

These days, many (but by no means all) people agree that the poems were written down in about 700 by a poet or poets who could write, but who had come out of an oral bardic tradition.

THE ILIAD: PLOT SUMMARY

Book 1: The god Apollo has sent a plague to the Greeks. To stop the deaths, the commander in chief, Agamemnon, must return a captive Trojan girl, daughter of the priest of Apollo. To avoid losing face, and as compensation for his loss, he demands Achilles, the best Greek fighter, hand over Briseis, another captive girl, to him. Achilles agrees but is furious. His mother, the sea goddess Thetis, persuades Zeus to punish the Greeks; and Achilles withdraws from the fighting.

Book 2: Zeus, complying with Thetis' request, sends Agamemnon a "false dream" telling him to attack Troy. As an ill-advised test of the troops' mettle, he announces that they are going home. Thersites, one of the ordinary soldiers, speaks out and is brutally silenced by Odysseus. The "catalog of ships"—the Greek forces are detailed.

Book 3: The Trojan prince Paris offers a challenge to single combat, which Menelaus accepts. In Troy, Helen hastens to the ramparts where she identifies the Greek champions for King Priam, a section known as the *teichoscopia*, or "viewing from the walls." Aphrodite spirits Paris away from the battlefield and reunites him with Helen.

Book 4: Athena is sent to the battlefield by Zeus. She incites the Trojan Pandarus to break the truce by shooting an arrow. Battle ensues. Menelaus is wounded.

Book 5: The Greek champion Diomedes is given a burst of strength by Athena. He wounds Aphrodite and Ares.

Book 6: Diomedes and Glaucus meet in battle, talk, and swap armor. The Trojans' main hope, Hector, goes into the city to instruct his mother, Hecuba, to dedicate a robe to Athena. He meets Paris and Helen, and finds his wife Andromache and their child Astyanax. She pleads with him to adopt a defensive position.

Book 7: Athena and the Trojan-favoring god Apollo decide to halt the fighting. Hector and Ajax are to fight a duel. The armies collect the dead and burn them. The Greeks decide to build a rampart to defend their ships.

Book 8: The gods assemble. Zeus threatens them: they must not intervene in the battle. Athena and Hera prepare to defy Zeus, but are prevented from doing so by Iris. Night falls over the armies.

Book 9: The embassy to Achilles: the Greek champions Phoenix, Ajax, and Odysseus set off to Achilles' tent to plead with him to rejoin the battle. He refuses.

Book 10: Agamemnon cannot sleep. Nestor suggests they need to gather intelligence. Meanwhile, Hector recruits a volunteer to scout the Greek camp—Dolon. Odysseus and Diomedes capture, interrogate, and kill him.

Book 11: More disaster for the Greeks. Diomedes, Odysseus, and Agamemnon are wounded. Achilles sends his companion Patroclus to Nestor's tent to enquire after the fate of the healer Machaon. Nestor reminisces about his glorious youth.

Book 12: Fighting around the Greek rampart. The Lycians Sarpedon (son of Zeus) and Glaucus lead the challenge. Hector breaches the gate.

Book 13: Zeus turns his attention elsewhere and Poseidon urges the Greeks on, gliding over the ocean in his chariot.

Book 14: Hera decides to distract Zeus, with the help of Sleep. She seduces him, and as he naps, the Greeks seize their chance.

Book 15: But Zeus wakes up. With Apollo urging him on, Hector breaches the Greek trench.

Book 16: In the face of this disaster, Achilles allows his friend Patroclus to fight, wearing his own precious armor. Patroclus kills Sarpedon. Patroclus beats the Trojans right back to Troy, but with Apollo's help, Hector finally kills him and takes Achilles' armor.

Book 17: The armies battle for possession of Patroclus' corpse. Achilles' horses weep. Menelaus and Ajax succeed in taking the body.

Book 18: Antilochus brings Achilles the bad news. Thetis goes to the god Hephaestus, who forges fresh armor for Achilles. The wondrous shield of Achilles is described.

Book 19: Morning: Achilles is still weeping, embracing Patroclus' body. Agamemnon acknowledges his mistake in demanding Briseis. Achilles arms for battle.

Book 20: As Achilles enters battle, Zeus sanctions the gods' involvement in the fighting. Achilles goes on the rampage, merciless, like a frenzied war god.

Book 21: Achilles gluts the river Scamander with Trojan corpses. The outraged river attacks Achilles. The gods fight each other: Hera boxes Artemis' ears.

Book 22: Achilles runs towards Troy. Hector, seeing him approach, takes flight. Achilles chases him three times around the city; they fight and Hector dies. Achilles attaches Hector's body to the back of his chariot. In Troy, the grief of Priam, Hecuba, and Andromache.

Book 23: Patroclus' ghost appears to Achilles: they must be buried together. Achilles sacrifices twelve Trojans on the funeral pyre. Achilles holds funeral games for Patroclus.

Book 24: Achilles cannot sleep. He drives his chariot, dragging Hector's body, around Patroclus' tomb. The gods decide that enough is enough. With Hermes' help, Priam enters the Greek camp and ransoms Hector's body; Priam and Achilles weep together. The Trojans mourn Hector.

THE ODYSSEY: PLOT SUMMARY

Book 1: The gods assemble. Athena pleads Odysseus' case—he is trapped on Calypso's island, long after the other heroes of the Trojan War have reached home. She sends Hermes to order Calypso to release Odysseus. Meanwhile, in disguise, she visits Odysseus' son Telemachus on Ithaca, and suggests he set out to find news of his father.

Book 2: Telemachus calls an assembly of the principal men of Ithaca—the first since Odysseus' departure. He berates the suitors who have been hassling his mother Penelope. Telemachus prepares a ship.

Book 3: Telemachus, with the disguised Athena, arrives in Pylos. King Nestor tells him of the return from Troy of Menelaus and Agamemnon.

Book 4: Telemachus arrives in Sparta, home of Menelaus and Helen. More war stories: Helen tells how Odysseus infiltrated Troy disguised as a beggar, and about the Wooden Horse. Menelaus says he hears Odysseus is held on Calypso's island. Back in Ithaca, the suitors plan to ambush Telemachus' ship.

Book 5: (Meanwhile . . .) Hermes arrives on Calypso's island; she reluctantly releases Odysseus. A storm at sea washes him up on an unknown shore.

Book 6: In the land of the Phaeacians, Nausicaa, prompted by a dream, sets out to wash her clothes in the river. There she meets the shipwrecked Odysseus.

Book 7: Odysseus, without revealing his identity, meets Nausicaa's parents, King Alcinous and Queen Arete.

Book 8: Alcinous arranges a feast. The bard Demodocus sings about the quarrel of Odysseus and Achilles. Alcinous organizes an athletics contest. Demodocus sings of the Wooden Horse. Odysseus weeps.

Book 9: Odysseus admits his identity. He tells the Phaeacians what happened after he left Troy: how he visited the land of the Lotus Eaters and the land of the Cyclops; how he foolishly told the Cyclops his name and earned the hatred of Poseidon (the creature's father).

Book 10: Odysseus' story continued: Aeolus; the cannibalistic Laestrygonians; the arrival on Circe's island; how she turns his men into hogs. He outwits her, and he and his men remain a year. Circe advises Odysseus he must visit the Underworld and consult the prophet Tiresias.

Book 11: Odysseus' story continued: the Underworld. Tiresias tells Odysseus: do not eat the cattle of Helios, the sun god. Odysseus meets his mother and the ghosts of Agamemnon, Achilles, Patroclus, Ajax, and Antilochus; he sees Tantalus, Sisyphus, Heracles, and others.

Book 12: Odysseus' story continued: the Sirens; and Scylla and Charybdis. They arrive on the island of the cattle of Helios. Odysseus' men foolishly decide to slaughter and eat some of the cattle. As they set out from the island all hands are lost in a storm, save Odysseus, who eventually washes up on Calypso's island. Odysseus' story ends.

Book 13: The Phaeacians assemble gifts for Odysseus and equip a ship. They put him down safely on Ithaca. Athena appears, disguises him as an ancient beggar and tells him to visit the swineherd Eumaeus.

Book 14: The loyal Eumaeus welcomes the disguised Odysseus, who gives a fictitious account of himself.

Book 15: Sparta: Athena tells Telemachus to get back home. Ithaca: Eumaeus and Odysseus yarn.

Book 16: Telemachus visits Eumaeus' hut and is reunited with his father. The pair plot how to overcome the suitors. Meanwhile, the suitors plot Telemachus' murder.

Book 17: Telemachus returns home and tells Penelope of the news gleaned on his travels—but not about Odysseus' reappearance. Odysseus arrives at the palace, still disguised as a beggar. His old dog Argos recognises him and dies. The suitors treat Odysseus with contempt.

Book 18: The suitors encourage a scrap between Odysseus and another beggar, Irus, whom the hero knocks out. The maid Melantho taunts Odysseus.

Book 19: In accordance with their plans, Telemachus quietly begins to stash away the palace's weapons. Penelope questions

Odysseus, who spins her a false yarn. While bathing his feet, the old nurse Eurycleia recognizes Odysseus. Odysseus swears her to silence.

Book 20: Penelope dreams Odysseus is lying beside her. A series of omens bodes ill for the suitors. More insults for Odysseus.

Book 21: Penelope challenges the suitors to string Odysseus' bow. All the suitors fail. Telemachus sends Penelope back to her quarters. Odysseus easily strings the bow.

Book 22: Odysseus turns the arrows on the suitors. With Telemachus' help, he slaughters them. Telemachus orders the disloyal maids to clear up the gore, then hangs them.

Book 23: Eurycleia tells Penelope that the beggar is Odysseus. Penelope tests him by ordering that their bed be brought out of doors. He proves his identity: it is their secret that the bed cannot be moved, since one of its bedposts is an olive tree. They weep, talk, and sleep together.

Book 24: The ghosts of the suitors arrive in the Underworld. Odysseus visits his aged father. The suitors' families prepare to avenge themselves on Odysseus, but Athena intervenes to prevent more bloodshed.

2. The living, the dead, and the deathless:
Mortality in Hesiod, Homer, and Sophocles

In the beginning . . . there was Chaos, which was a dark chasm of nothingness; and the Earth; and the sepulchral depths of Tartarus. And Eros: desire, the urge to change and generate, was always there. Night and Day were born from Chaos, and Heaven was born from Earth. Heaven and Earth became the parents of Ocean, Cronus, Rhea, and Tethys, who lives on the seabed.

With a reaping hook, Cronus lopped off his father's genitals and flung them into the sea. From the drops of blood that fell on the earth came the Giants; and from the sea foam, into which the genitals had plunged, was born Aphrodite, sex goddess. Cronus and his sister Rhea had children: Hestia, who guards the hearth; Demeter, the harvest goddess; Poseidon, ruler of the sea, and Hades, king of the Underworld. Cronus, in angry jealousy, ate his own children—though when it came to his youngest, Zeus' turn, Rhea substituted a rock. Choking, he vomited up his other offspring.

The Olympian gods—Zeus and his siblings—now battled with the Titans, the older gods, Cronus and Rhea and the rest. Finally the Olympians won out, and locked away the older gods deep in Tartarus. Zeus became king of the gods. Among his children were

Athena; the Fates Clotho, Lachesis, and Atropos; and the Graces. Demeter bore him Persephone; Leto bore him Apollo and Artemis; his sister Hera bore him Hebe and Ares. Hephaestus, Hera produced without a father.

This is a (very abridged) account of the *Theogony*, a genealogy of the gods and creation myth by the poet Hesiod, who was writing roughly around the time the Homeric epics were coming into being, probably sometime in the eighth century. (There have long been arguments, still unresolved, about which came first, the works of Homer or the works of Hesiod.) The *Theogony* is a curious poem, infused with influences from the Near East, and with parallels to Akkadian and Hittite texts. And, while it would be unfair to call it crude, exactly, it's certainly not a sustained, sophisticated masterpiece in the manner of the *Iliad*. Unusually for such an early poet, we know quite a lot about Hesiod, because he talks about himself in his works (his other poem is called *Works and Days*, and is a sort of farming-manual-cum-moral-guide). We know, for instance, that he tended sheep on the slopes of Mount Helicon in Boeotia, a peak sacred to the Muses; that he'd once won a prize for singing at Chalcis, and that he felt that his brother Perses had diddled him out of his fair share of inheritance. He was a peasant farmer, in a world ruled by aristocrats.

If you look at a modern retelling of Greek myths, the chances are that it will begin, as I began this chapter, with a romp through the *Theogony*, which, with *Works and Days*, is a hugely important source for mythological stories. But the thing about these tales is that they are malleable. There is no one "book of myths" in ancient Greece, a holy bible of authorized versions. What we think of as the Greek myths—all the good stuff about the labors of Heracles, Oedipus and the Sphinx, and a hundred other yarns—have found their way down to us because the stories are woven into Greek literature and art: and as such they were, naturally, subject to different treatment and interpretation by different writers and artists. For instance, mythical stories were the raw material used by Greek tragic playwrights in the fifth century: there were very few tragedies that dealt directly with current events. The most famous telling of Oedipus' story is in Sophocles' play *Oedipus the King*; and, to suit his own dramatic purpose, Sophocles gave him very modern qualities and used the story as a way of touching on contemporary Athenian politics. So the tone of mythical stories can feel very different, depending on the context in which they are found. The *Theogony*, with its incestuous couplings and phalanxes of weird creatures, seems a million miles away from Sophocles' rational, inquiring Oedipus.

Frequently, too, there are various versions of the "same" myth. Take the story of Medea, who helped Jason get hold of the Golden Fleece. She was furious when he decided to leave her and take a new wife, Glauce, daughter of Creon, king of Corinth. In revenge, Medea killed Creon and fled the city, leaving her children behind; they were killed by the Corinthians in turn. Or *is* that what happened? In Euripides' play about Medea, she kills Glauce with a poisoned robe and crown that burns her flesh, murders her own children in order to punish their father, and escapes to Athens in the flying chariot belonging to her grandfather, the sun god, Helios. (A most amazing scene, brilliantly done in London and on Broadway in 1992 in Jonathan Kent's production, with Diana Rigg in the title role.) There was a rumor in antiquity that Euripides had taken a bribe from the Corinthians to change the ending; but his version is no less of a "Greek myth" for all that.

So what do these myths have in common? Well, for me, one of the most exciting things about these stories—apart from the fact that they are wonderful tales that are a pleasure to encounter— is that they confront perhaps the biggest question of all: what it means to be human, what it means to be mortal. What the Greek myths share is that they present a world in which people and gods freely mingle (or at least in which the gods' power is always near at hand). And there is something very particular about these Greek gods of myth. They are like us. They look like us (even though if you saw one undisguised you would be burned up in their white-hot brilliance, as happened to the mortal Semele when she asked to look at Zeus). The gods have human foibles and failings (you've only got to look at the stories about Hera, the archetypal jealous wife, or about Zeus, the archetypal philandering husband, to get a sense of that). But . . . they are inexorably powerful, wielding that power in often cruel or senseless ways. And they cannot die. So they are, at once, both like and unlike us; and it is by sensing this dialectic between mortal and immortal that we can start to perceive man—and the human condition—more clearly.

The summation of this idea is in the *Iliad*. Book 1 sets out its terms with great clarity and economy, introducing us both to the main characters and to the two main locations: the plain outside Troy and Mount Olympus, home of the gods. A reminder of the first few lines:

> Rage—Goddess, sing the rage of Peleus' son Achilles,
> murderous, doomed, that cost the Achaeans countless losses,
> hurling down to the House of Death so many sturdy souls,
> great fighters' souls, but made their bodies carrion,
> feasts for the dogs and birds,
> and the will of Zeus was moving towards its end.
>
> *Iliad* 1 1–6

The rage of Achilles; the death of countless heroes; the will of Zeus being fulfilled—these lines are a neat indication of what's to come in the rest of the poem. The ensuing narrative of Book 1 describes what caused Achilles' wrath (that pride-fueled row with his commander in chief, Agamemnon); and how Achilles persuaded his mother, the goddess Thetis, to get Zeus to rain destruction down on the Greeks to avenge his dishonor. The scene finally moves from the Greek camp to Mount Olympus. The gods feast, they drink nectar, and they enjoy a joke: "uncontrollable laughter broke from the happy gods / as they watched the god of fire breathing hard / and bustling through the halls."

The Greek camp, and the gods' celestial home: two worlds, and how different they are. The men, whose deaths are coming thick and fast; whose corpses will be made carrion. The Olympians, in their lofty halls, who squabble and smile and joke. This contrast is crucial to the poem: for what is right at the heart of the *Iliad* is its head-on confrontation with the idea of mortality. And the most distinctive way that you can talk about the meaning of mortality is to contrast it with immortality: short, furious, burning-bright lives set alongside existences that are endless.

One thing that we need to understand is that in the world of Homer, mortal life is . . . it. There's no Christian-style heaven awaiting the heroes, nowhere for earthly virtue to be rewarded by an eternity of bliss. The souls of the dead do have an existence of sorts in the Underworld, but it's not exactly a place you'd want to be. In Book 11 of the *Odyssey*, the hero visits it, and it's rather a horrifying spectacle: the dead are miserable, helpless wraiths who can summon up a conversation only after they have drunk the blood of the animals Odysseus has sacrificed. Achilles' ghost tells Odysseus that he'd rather be a lowly slave to a dirt-poor tenant farmer than be even king of the dead. In *Iliad* Book 20, the "dank, mouldering horrors" of the houses of the dead are said to make even the gods shudder.

So the short, bright lives of the heroes are what matter, not what happens to them afterwards. When men die in the *Iliad*—which they do, page after page of them, many invented just so that we can see them fall—they do so unwillingly, horrifically. When Patroclus is downed by Hector in Book 16,

Death cut him short. The end closed in around him.
Flying free of his limbs
his soul went winging down to the House of Death
wailing his fate, leaving his manhood far behind,
his young and supple strength.

Iliad 16 1001–1005

If flesh is a kind of prison in Christian thought, bogging us
down with its appetites and desires, then the opposite is true in
Homer: we are nothing without our beating hearts, our "young and
supple strength."

And yet . . . there is a sort of immortality that is terribly important to these men: their fame, their glory as fighters, which lives on
after them. Their payoff for a life cut short is this immortality of
renown. As usual, it is Achilles, with his hotline to the supernatural,
who puts this most articulately:

"Mother tells me,
the immortal goddess Thetis with her glistening feet,
that two fates bear me on to the day of death.
If I hold out here and I lay siege to Troy,
my journey home is gone, but my glory never dies.
If I voyage back to the fatherland I love,
my pride, my glory dies . . .
true, but the life that's left me will be long,
the stroke of death will not come on me quickly."

Iliad 9 497–505

So what are the gods all about? First, one needs to remove all
thought of a redemptive, benign deity such as that of Christian tradition. The gods in Homer are quarrelsome and petty; protective and
tender; magnificent, implacable, and terrifying—occasionally ridic-

ulous, and, in fact, the chief providers of comic relief in the poem. Zeus, king of the gods, is far and away the most powerful of them: as he tells the other Olympians (rather bizarrely), if they all stood on the earth and tried to drag him down from heaven in a tug of war, he'd easily be able to pull them all back up again. His "will," referred to in those opening lines, is that Troy will eventually fall; and in the short term, that the Greeks will suffer humiliation in order to satisfy Achilles' injured pride. Nonetheless, the other gods do their best to outwit Zeus, and occasionally succeed: there's an amazing and very funny episode in Book 14 when Hera dresses up in her sexiest outfit and seduces Zeus so that, during his postcoital nap, she can get her own way for a while.

The gods care about what happens to the heroes. They watch what's going on intently. A number of heroes, including Hector and Patroclus, are repeatedly called "dear to Zeus"—his fondness, however, does not prevent their deaths. The gods take sides: Hera, Athena, and Poseidon are pro-Greek; Apollo, Artemis, and Ares are pro-Trojan. Sometimes they take the field to help along their favorite heroes: in Book 5, Athena gives the warrior Diomedes a huge surge of power so that he even manages to wound Ares—though, says Homer, he heals "as quickly as fresh fig-juice curdles milk." Diomedes wounds Aphrodite, too; horrified, she rushes off to her mother, Dione, in tears. The battle is life or death to the heroes on the field . . . but Aphrodite is like a child with a grazed knee. In other words, since the gods cannot experience death, the war, while it is certainly consuming, is quite a different business for them than it is for the mortals.

Not that they aren't emotionally affected. Some of the gods have close ties to men: Thetis is the mother of Achilles; Zeus is the father of Sarpedon. It's a terrible business, that an immortal should love a mortal when, as Glaucus tells Diomedes in Book 6:

"Like the generations of leaves, the lives of mortal men.
Now the wind scatters the old leaves across the earth,
now the living timber bursts with the new buds
and spring comes round again. And so with men:
as one generation comes to life, another dies away."

Iliad 6 170–4

For the gods, these beloved creatures are born and dead in a mere blink of an eye. It is a heart-wrenching moment when Zeus has to watch his own son Sarpedon succumb on the battlefield. He says to Hera:

"My cruel fate . . .
my Sarpedon, the man I love the most, my own son—
doomed to die at the hands of Menoetius' son Patroclus.
My heart is torn in two as I try to weigh all this.
Shall I pluck him up, now, while he's still alive
and set him down in the rich green land of Lycia,
far from the war at Troy and all its tears?"

Iliad 16 514–20

Hera persuades him not to. Zeus agrees, "But he showered tears of blood that drenched the earth, / showers in praise of him, his own dear son, / the man Patroclus was just about to kill / on Troy's fertile soil, far from his fatherland."

It is Achilles who seems fully to grasp the brutal reality of his own—and others'—mortality. In the thick of his berserking anger and grief after the death of Patroclus, he takes on a son of Priam, Lycaon, who grasps his knees in supplication and begs for his life. Achilles answers him:

"Come friend, you too must die. Why moan about it so?
Even Patroclus died, a far, far better man than you.

And look, you see how handsome and powerful I am?
The son of a great man, the mother who gave me life
a deathless goddess. But even for me, I tell you,
death and the strong force of fate are waiting.
There will come a dawn or sunset or high noon
when a man will take my life in battle too—
flinging a spear perhaps
or whipping a deadly arrow off his bow."

Iliad 20 118–12

Lycaon's end is inevitable—because all men die, and because, at this fateful moment, he has met Achilles, the stronger man, the implacable death-bringer. A few lines after this passage young Lycaon is a corpse sprawled face down in the dust, then Achilles flings him, triumphantly, grotesquely, into the river. But Achilles is right. Soon it will be his turn—and it will be an arrow, not a spear. Men are wretched, yes. But compared with the steady—and somehow meaningless—beam of the gods' endless existence, the lives of men, like shooting stars, are brief but beautiful, bright, and intense.

Homer's theology did not go unchallenged by later writers. His depiction of the gods as capricious, imperfect, even childlike creatures was attacked as fanciful or immoral by some thinkers, notably Plato. Xenophanes, a poet-philosopher who was born in Ionia (modern Turkey) in about 520, famously wrote: "Homer and Hesiod have attributed to the gods all things that are shameful and blameworthy among men: stealing, adultery, and deceiving each other." He mocked the way in which poets and artists produced anthropomorphic gods that looked rather like themselves: if horses could produce artworks, he said, horses would draw gods that looked like horses. The intellectual revolution of the fifth century saw man placed more firmly at the center of the universe, the relationship between humanity and the divine subjected to rigorous philosophical inquiry and skepticism. The gods and religion were still right at the heart of Athenian civic and political life. But works such as Thucydides' *History of the Peloponnesian War*, for example, set great events firmly in the context of human actions and desires. It is not the gods who ensure Athens' defeat in the war against Sparta, according to Thucydides, it is the Athenians' own, human mistakes. "Man is the measure of all things" is the famous saying attributed to the philosopher Protagoras.

The great dramas that survive from fifth-century Athens reflect this intellectual enlightenment: its debates, controversies, arguments, and, sometimes, limitations. Sophocles was born in 496 at Colonus, near Athens, and lived till he was 90. He wrote over a hundred plays for the Athenian stage—for the great festivals, particularly the springtime City Dionysia, which saw three playwrights, over as many days, stage a tragic trilogy and a comedic satyr play. (More on these festivals in chapter 3.) The centrality of man, his teeming inventiveness, the power of his mind that has seen him develop from lowly farmer to city-dwelling, law-making rationalist, is memorably articulated in the most famous chorus from Sophocles' play *Antigone*, produced in about 441:

> Numberless wonders
> terrible wonders walk the earth but none the match for man—
> that great wonder crossing the heaving grey sea,
> driven on by the blasts of winter
> on through breakers crashing left and right,
> holds his steady course
> and the oldest of the gods he wears away—
> the Earth, the immortal, the inexhaustible—
> as his ploughs go back and forth, year in, year out
> with the breed of stallions turning up the furrows

. . . Man the master, ingenious past all measure
past all dreams, the skills within his grasp
      he forges on, now to destruction
now again to greatness . . .

                    Antigone 376–385; 406–409
                    Translation: Robert Fagles

Man has tamed nature. (Wearing away the earth may strike us as somewhat sinister in these days of environmental anxiety, but for humans living half a millennium before the birth of Christ, to make any kind of impact on the hostile landscape of Greece was a triumph.) Human ingenuity, in fact, can do more or less anything—but, hints this chorus, it can bring "destruction" as well as "greatness." In the play, Antigone is condemned to death by her uncle Creon, the king of Thebes, because she decides to go against his command not to bury the body of her brother, who fought against the city and was defeated. This is her "reckless daring," which has transgressed the "laws of the land." However, unsurprisingly, the course of the play is not straightforward: man-made law and the strictures of the gods appear to be in conflict. Creon's punishment of his niece leads to the suicide of his son, who is Antigone's fiancé, and also that of his own wife: the gods come down heavily on Creon in the end, even though he can be seen to represent the sort of rational, civic virtues idealized in fifth-century Athens.

Perhaps the ultimate articulation, though, of the ambiguous power of man's penetrating intelligence is Sophocles' most famous play, *Oedipus the King*. As I mentioned earlier, despite the fact that it is set in the mythical past, and despite the fact that there is a scary Hesiod-style Sphinx lurking in the backstory, *Oedipus the King* is a very modern drama. What happens is this: A plague is causing havoc in Thebes. Oedipus, the king—a good man, respected by his people—is eager to discover what's caused it. So he sends his brother-in-law Creon to consult the oracle at Delphi. (This is the same Creon as the king in *Antigone*, though one mustn't imagine that these mythical figures are given the same characters in different plays.) Creon returns with the news that the plague can be stopped only if the murderer of the former king of Thebes, Laius, can be found and killed or exiled. Now, Laius died some years back, before Oedipus, a Corinthian, turned up in Thebes. He was made king after he successfully solved the riddle of the Sphinx and freed the city from the dreadful creature's curse.

The play now quickly becomes a detective story: the first and, perhaps, the greatest detective story. Oedipus is a man of steely intelligence and decisive action (a bit like the ideal Athenian as described by Pericles in his funeral oration in Thucydides—of which more in chapter 3). Why wasn't the crime investigated at the time? he inquires testily, as if he were the new commissioner of police. Because our attention was diverted by the Sphinx, comes the answer. Well, the crime is jolly well going to get solved now. Oedipus is in the mood to get things done.

First, he sends for the blind prophet Tiresias. "You are the murderer you hunt," the old man disconcertingly informs the baffled—and in due course very angry—Oedipus. "Riddles—all you can say are riddles," says Oedipus. "Ah, but aren't you the best man alive at solving riddles?" replies the prophet.

Oedipus begins to suspect that Tiresias is plotting with Creon to ruin his reputation and depose him. Oedipus' wife, Jocasta—previously married to Laius—appears, with a reassuring angle: prophecy is all a lot of nonsense, take no notice. After all, there was once a prophecy that Laius would be killed by his own son, and *that* never happened. Laius and I, she says, had a child, and he was exposed as a baby on the mountainside and died. Laius was not killed by his son, but by thieves, at a place where three roads meet.

What's that, says Oedipus—a place where three roads meet?

Why did no one ever mention that detail before? His mind is full of misgivings. He sends for the sole survivor of Laius' entourage, who is now a shepherd. It suddenly becomes very important to get an eyewitness to clear up that issue: was Laius killed by a gang of thieves, as everyone keeps saying, or by a man on his own? Oedipus tells Jocasta his fears—he once had an argument with a man at a place where three roads meet, years ago, before he ever came to Thebes, and killed him. In telling this story he explains why he was traveling. He is the son of the king and queen of Corinth, Polybus and Merope, but as a young man he heard insulting rumors that he was not the true child of the king. To clear up the mystery, he asked the Delphic oracle, who, giving a typically indirect answer, told him that he was fated to kill his father and marry his mother. So Oedipus fled Corinth, terrified the awful prediction would come true . . . and it was after that that he had an argument with the man at the crossroads . . .

Out of the blue a messenger now arrives, bringing the news that Polybus of Corinth is dead. Sad news though it is, in some ways it is a relief: Oedipus certainly did not kill him, and so the prophecy must have been false. Still, there's always the chance that he will end up sleeping with his mother. Jocasta again tries to reassure him: our lives are governed by chance, not oracles. Many men have dreamed they have slept with their mothers. There is nothing to fear. Indeed there isn't, says the messenger. You really do have nothing to fear: because Merope was not in fact your mother.

Oedipus, shocked, realizes he has another witness to cross-examine. The messenger reveals that he himself gave Oedipus, as a baby, to Polybus and Merope. And he, the messenger, was given the baby Oedipus in turn by another man, a Theban. It seems horribly inevitable that that witness, the Theban, is the same shepherd whom they have already summoned, the one who was on the scene when Laius was murdered.

Quite suddenly Jocasta changes tack—she tries to get Oedipus to stop his questioning. Oedipus laughs at her: he thinks she's worried about discovering that he is of low birth. She silently goes into the palace. The shepherd arrives. With extreme reluctance, he submits to Oedipus' questioning, and admits that many years ago a baby was given him by Jocasta and Laius to be exposed and killed; for a prophecy had warned the baby would end up killing his parents.

Suddenly, with dreadful clarity, it all comes together in Oedipus' mind. He was the baby Laius and Jocasta sent to be exposed, who was rescued by the shepherd and handed to the Corinthian, who in turn passed him on to Polybus and Merope. He was the man who killed Laius, his own father, in an argument on the road; and the one that married his own mother and fathered her children.

> "O god—
> all come true, all burst to light!
> O light—now let me look my last on you!
> I stand revealed at last—
> cursed in my birth, cursed in marriage,
> cursed in the lives I cut down with these hands!"
>
> *Oedipus the King* 1306–1310
> Translation: Robert Fagles

He leaves the stage and enters the palace, into which Jocasta disappeared earlier. Later, a messenger recounts what happened inside the palace: Jocasta hanged herself, and Oedipus, taking the brooches from her dress, gouged out his own eyes. Blinded and bloody, Oedipus finally emerges on stage again. His self-mutilation is grotesquely appropriate. He could not see: now he cannot see.

The ghastly logic with which all this is revealed is one of the things that makes this play so powerful. Oedipus starts by asking a question: how can we stop the plague? That inexorably turns into: who killed Laius? and, then: who am I? The answer to every question is "Oedipus." And of course, he answers every question with deadly accuracy: he is very good at this kind of work, as Tiresias, the blind prophet, pointed out.

The riddle that Oedipus solved, saving Thebes from the Sphinx's curse was this: what walks on four legs, two legs, three legs? The answer is: man. As a child he crawls on four legs; as a man he walks on two; and in old age he has a third, a stick. At the end of the play, Oedipus, the blind man, will need to rely on a stick. The answer to the Sphinx's riddle could as well be "Oedipus." Man is Oedipus; Oedipus is man.

There's no easy moral embedded in this play. There's nothing to suggest that Oedipus is being punished for some sin, for displaying overweening hubris, for failing to honor the gods. In this worldview there is no god hurling thunderbolts at Oedipus, in the way that the offended Poseidon sends storms to thwart Odysseus in Homer. But just as in the *Odyssey*—which of course also has a supremely resourceful, clever hero at its heart—there are things that man, with all his intelligence, cannot conquer or account for. Perhaps the point is, as the last line of the play suggests, that we should "count no man happy till he dies"—that, like Oedipus, none of us can afford to imagine that our lives, our circumstances, our happiness, are secure. Yes, the storytelling of this play, the cruelly neat unfolding of the drama, accounts for much of its power. But it also grips us, two and a half thousand years after its creation, because it seems to capture something that is still true, and frightening, about the human condition. We think of human intellect as an all-conquering, inexorable force, godlike even. And yet we are all too mortal: the mind's power can be dashed at a stroke. We look like gods, but we are not gods.

Still, there is a chink of hope. At the end of the play, Oedipus has nothing. He is an outcast, an exile, a polluted creature who has committed dreadful, unspeakable crimes. But perhaps, for everything that he has lost, he has gained one thing: the beginnings of self-knowledge.

3. Man is a political animal:
Democracy and the *polis*

ACCORDING TO ARISTOTLE, in the *Politics*, "Man is by nature a political animal." Thanks to a trick of (mis)translation, this is a phrase that is usually splendidly misapplied. It does not mean that human beings have evolved especially so they can run for election in the local council. Still less does it mean that humans can't help themselves cooking up all kinds of skulduggery by the office water-cooler. What Aristotle said was that man was by nature *politikos*, which is the Greek adjective relating to the noun *polis*. *Polis* (plural: *poleis*) is often translated, rather clumsily, as "city-state." What Aristotle is saying, then, is that "man by nature is an animal fitted for living in a *polis*." In his *Inquiry Concerning Animals* (see chapter 7), Aristotle says that other creatures, not just humans, are *politikoi*: ants, cranes, wasps, and bees—in other words, animals that live in "communities." What makes humans different from these other "political animals," says Aristotle, is that they are capable of making decisions, they are "deliberative."

So what is a *polis*, then? Well, in the ancient Greek world there were over a thousand of them. Athens was one, Sparta another: these were the political, social, and community units into which life was organized. They could include not just the urban settlement from which they took their name, but the surrounding hinterland—in Athens' case, Attica. They were basically self-governing, though they might forge alliances with each other or, as often as not, be at war with each other.

In the account of the Persian Wars by the historian Herodotus (of which more in chapter 5), there is an episode, after the battle of Salamis, in which Xerxes, ruler of the mighty Persian empire, sends messengers to Athens suggesting that they come to terms. The Athenians refuse, but also send a message to reassure an understandably jittery Sparta, their ally, explaining just why they would never join forces with Xerxes:

> . . . we are all Greeks—one race speaking one language, with temples to the gods and religious rites in common, and with a common way of life.

> *Histories* 8 144
> Translation: Robin Waterfield

What Herodotus puts into the Athenians' mouths looks very much like a later ideological line being pitched back on to the 480s—in the thick of the wars at that time, it's unlikely the Greek cities were thinking about narratives of pan-Hellenic identity above the urgent business of saving their own skin. Nonetheless, it is interesting what the Athenians *don't* say is a defining Greek characteristic: there is nothing here about sharing a democratic political system. The reason the Athenians make this omission is, of course, because the Greek *poleis* were by no means uniformly democratic.

So, when we think about ancient Greece as the cradle of democracy, it's worth remembering that for every *polis* there was a differently shaded political system, ranging from single-person rule to oligarchy (literally, "rule by a few") to radical democracy (literally, "power of the people"). Athens' radical democratic constitution was the exception, rather than the rule. And, perhaps more importantly, it is also worth remembering that what we regard as democracy would probably not have been recognized as such by an Athenian citizen, were you magically to transport him from fifth-century Athens to modern Westminster or Washington. In fact, one eminent ancient historian has suggested that your hypothetical ancient Athenian would probably identify our democracies as a form of oligarchy.

Here's another suggestion of what a *polis* was—or at least the *polis* of Athens, in 413, as sketched by Thucydides in Book 7 of his *History of the Peloponnesian War*. The Athenians have just been utterly crushed by the Spartans at the battle of Syracuse, and face being entirely cut off on enemy territory. "No Hellenic army had ever suffered such as reverse. They had come to enslave others, and now they were going away frightened of being enslaved themselves . . ." The Athenian general, Nicias, tries to buck up the troops, no mean task:

> In a word, soldiers, you must make up your minds that to be brave now is a matter of necessity, since no place exists near at hand where a coward can take refuge, and that, if you escape the enemy now, you will all see again the homes for which you long, and the Athenians among you will build up again the great power of Athens, fallen though it is. It is men who make the city [*polis*], and not walls or ships with no men inside them.
>
> *History of the Peloponnesian War* 7 77
> Translation: Rex Warner

It is not its constitution, nor its geographical location, nor its particular manifestation through buildings and architecture that makes the *polis*: it is the citizens, the people themselves: a formulation that I find incredibly powerful, moving even.

How was democracy born? How did a city in Greece two and a half thousand years ago come to the extraordinary conclusion that it ought to be ruled by placing political power in the hands of its citizens? Let's go a long way back. If you read the *Iliad* or the *Odyssey*, what you figure out is that the Greeks are a loose network of allies, each with their king or leader, such that Odysseus is the royal ruler of Ithaca, for instance. In the *Odyssey*, Ithaca has an Assembly, a meeting of the leading local figures, at which Odysseus' son Telemachus speaks, though it is not quite clear what power the Assembly wields. In the eighth century, the time the *Iliad* and the *Odyssey* were probably composed, this kingship system already seems to represent the distant past. Hesiod, for instance, also composing in the eighth century, but in his case alluding to contemporary reality, hints that his agrarian society is dominated by a ruling aristocracy—and this was probably the prevailing pattern through the Greek world at the time.

In the seventh and sixth centuries, something else distinctive emerges: the rise of "tyrants" in various *poleis*. Again, don't be tricked by the English word: these figures weren't necessarily Pol Pot characters, enforcing reigns of terror; they were aristocrats, more like, who seized sole power after a struggle between rival factions, and, though we hear of brutality, this is not their defining characteristic. In Athens, one Cylon, a member of the aristocratic Alcmaeonid family, attempted to seize sole power in around 632 but failed; a decade afterwards Draco's code of laws was posted in Athens. (In later years it was said that nearly every offense carried the death penalty, hence our word "draconian.") In 594/3 Solon, the man later regarded as the grandfather of democracy, repealed all Draco's laws except for that dealing with homicide, and instituted a raft of reforms. He canceled all debts, relieving the poorer Attic farmers of economic burdens that had seen them securing loans on their own bodies, and thus virtually enslaved. He also organized the Athenians into four property classes that were made the basis of political rights, breaking the monopoly of the aristocrats; and he strengthened the popular

Assembly. We know about Solon from his own poetry alluding to these reforms. Solon points out that they pleased no one—the aristocrats were bitter that their privileges had been limited, the poorer farmers dissatisfied at the level of land and wealth redistribution.

Fifty years later, Athens got its tyrant, in the form of Pisistratus, another aristocrat, who, after two short-lived attempts on Athens and a period of exile, held power from 546/5, passing it on to his son Hippias in 528/7. Paradoxically, given what we understand by the word "tyrant," his stint running the show may have helped create stability and consolidated Solon's reforms, since he worked more or less within them (of course ensuring that his pals got the top jobs). In 514, however, Hippias' brother Hipparchus was assassinated by the famous tyrannicides, the lovers Harmodius and Aristogiton. Far from striking a conscious blow for *liberté*, *egalité*, and *fraternité*, Aristogiton was in fact punishing Hipparchus for trying to steal his boyfriend: never mind, for the lovers were later honored as heroes and had a wonderful statue erected to commemorate their famous deed. Hippias' regime got a bit tougher after this episode, but was finally put down in 510 with Spartan aid. More faction-fighting followed, this time between Isagoras, another noble with oligarchic, possibly tyrannical tendencies, and the equally aristocratic Cleisthenes, another member of the Alcmaeonid family.

As far as Herodotus was concerned, Cleisthenes was the true founder of Athenian democracy. Yet again, we know of no high-minded belief that bringing power to the people was the "right" thing to do. Giving the ordinary people power in order to help defeat his political rivals, achieve stability, and possibly fend off another tyranny was a practical and pragmatic, if astoundingly bold, move. Anyway, no one called it at democracy in 508/7, when he pushed through his reforms. The buzz words of the time were *isegoria*—freedom of speech; and *isonomia*—equality before the law. Cleisthenes divided Attica into three broad areas: city, inland, and coast. Demes (villages or wards) from each of these three areas were combined to create ten new tribes, which formed the focus of the selection of various officials and the running of the army. This system weakened purely regional loyalties, which may have been adding to Athens' internal tensions. Each "tribe" had its own religious hero-cult (in which a mythical or real mortal was accorded semi-divine status). Fifty citizens from each tribe, chosen by lot, formed what was called the Council of 500. Its main task was to prepare business for the Assembly, which any citizen man could attend and vote in, and which was the main legislative body (in practice it is estimated that around 5,000 men would physically have had room to meet at the Assembly, out of an estimated 30,000 citizens). The lottery also chose the 6,000 men who became potential jurors in any given year; a hearing could end up with at least 501 jurors. To Cleisthenes was also attributed the creation annually of a board of ten generals, and the institution of ostracism, the process by which an unpopular or politically dangerous citizen could be banished for ten years: in this system each voter would write down the name of the man he wished to banish on an *ostrakon*, a potsherd, whence our word ostracism. A bit later down the line, in 487/6, selection by lot replaced election of the nine archons, who were responsible for legal matters and religious festivals. In fact, the lottery was the selection route for most officials of Athens, barring the powerful board of ten generals, who were elected. In 462/1, finally, the Areopagus, an ancient council of ex-archons with certain judicial powers, was downgraded to a homicide court by the reforms of Ephialtes and Pericles. The latter—what a coincidence—was yet another member, through his mother, of the Alcmaeonid family; you can see, then, that this ultra-fair lottery system did not rule out continued aristocratic power, especially as the elected board of generals became extremely important. Pericles was elected to the generalship annually between 443 and 429. This Athenian democracy, then, was a very different beast from our modern democracies in Britain or the US—

the latter, anyway, inspired less by radical Athenian democracy than by the Republic of Rome—what with its Senate and Capitol . . .

If the invention of democracy started as a pragmatic move, it retrospectively became an ideal. Pericles' funeral oration in Thucydides' *Peloponnesian War* puts it movingly:

> Our constitution is called a democracy because power is in the hands not of a minority but of the whole people. When it is a question of settling private disputes, everyone is equal before the law; when it is a question of putting one person before another in positions of public responsibility, what counts is not membership of a particular class, but the actual ability which the man possesses. No one, so long as he has it in him to be of service to the state, is kept in political obscurity because of poverty.
>
> *History of the Peloponnesian War* 2 37
> Translation: Rex Warner

Before we get too bleary-eyed about this undeniably stirring rhetoric it might be worth remembering for a moment that "the whole people" meant adult, male citizens. Women, the entire slave population, and foreigners had no political powers and did not participate in this equality. There were probably around 30,000 Athenian male citizens; and about 300,000–400,000 in the population a whole, including around 100,000 slaves.

SPARTA

If Athens' democracy was one way to solve the problem of feuding aristocrats, then Sparta came up with another: an oligarchy entirely unique in Greece, and regarded by outsiders with wonder, curiosity, and a frisson of fear. The Spartans said that their constitution had been given them by one Lycurgus, a semi-mythical figure. Power was held by a body of thirty called the *gerousia* (elders), which included the two kings of Sparta. The other members were aged at least sixty. (Sparta was thus in some ways a gerontocracy.) The *gerousia* had the function of a supreme court, and could overturn decisions reached by the Assembly, which consisted of all adult male citizens, who were called the *homoioi* (similars). A board of five men called ephors, who were elected annually, wielded chief executive power, and exercised general control over the kings' conduct, settling disputes between them if necessary (and it seems that it fairly frequently was necessary). The Spartan state had one thing at its heart: militarism. Boys (if they had been deemed sufficiently hardy newborns not to have been cast into a pit outside the city in an initial round of infanticide) were removed from their families at age seven and passed into the *agoge* (upbringing), which was in the charge of a guardian known as the *paidonomos* (boy-herd). Until the age of eighteen they were organized into "packs" and "herds" and trained as fighters, a process involving brutal physical ordeals. In addition, boys aged twelve and upward were supposed to receive a young adult as their "inspirer," a relationship that combined friendship, teaching, and, perhaps, sex. The most talented boys, as they reached adulthood, were selected to join a secret band of warriors called the *crypteia*, who infiltrated Helot territory and murdered troublemakers. The Helots were the Spartans' slaves: peoples of the neighboring Greek states of Messenia and Laconia, who had been conquered by the Spartan military machine. (There was a frequent threat of Helot uprising, and the Spartans ritually declared war on them each year.) These subject peoples provided the economic basis of the Spartan state, freeing up the *homoioi* to focus absolutely on military matters and to maintain the only truly professional army in the Greek world. And it was a sort of circular system: in turn, the professional militarism of the *homoioi* was necessary to keep in check the enslaved populations on which Spartan supremacy relied.

There's a marvelous passage in Herodotus that counts as the first-ever piece of political theoretical debate. It takes place after the false successor of King Cambyses of Persia has been deposed by a group of nobles, including the future king Darius. In a hilariously unlikely, but utterly fascinating passage, Herodotus has the conspirators sit down, roll up their sleeves, and debate what is the best form of constitution.

One of the conspirators, Otanes, speaks first in favor of democracy:

> In the first place it has the best of all names to describe it: equality before the law. In the second place, it is entirely free of the vices of monarchy. It is government by lot, it is accountable government, and it refers all decisions to the common people.
>
> Herodotus 3 80
> Translation: Robin Waterfield

Megabyzus then speaks in favor of oligarchy (by way of arguing against democracy): "A mob is ineffective, and there is nothing more stupid or more given to brutality," he says. ". . . The approach of the general populace is that of a river swollen with winter rain: they rush blindly forward and sweep things before them." Finally, Darius speaks out in favor of monarchy (surprise, surprise, the Persian system, which, of course, they were in no danger of dropping):

> If you have a single person, and he is the best person in the world, how could you hope to improve on that? . . . In an oligarchy, however, a number of people are trying to benefit the community, and in this situation violent personal feuds tend to arise . . .
>
> Herodotus 3 82
> Translation: Robin Waterfield

He continues by saying that monarchy tends to emerge from such oligarchic feuds; and in a democratic system, a "champion of the people," also a virtual king, tends to emerge to put an end to the inevitable corruption in a democracy. This, he claims, is "proof that monarchy is the best system." Not only is this debate interesting in the rather sensible critiques it puts forward of its three chosen political systems, but it is an insight into the sort of arguments that may have been current in fifth-century Athens and elsewhere: democracy was certainly not short of its critics.

Thucydides gives a fascinating insight into Athenian democracy in action: an example of the Assembly, to paraphrase Herodotus, rushing forward and sweeping things before them. In 427, during the Peloponnesian War, the Assembly made the decision to punish the inhabitants of Mytilene on Lesbos for revolting against their Athenian masters: they ordered the execution of all the men and the enslavement of all the women and children. Overnight, though, people began to have second thoughts, and an emergency Assembly meeting was called for the next day. Thucydides has the two sides—death and mercy—represented by a pair of brilliant speeches. Mercy wins the day. Then comes a remarkable passage in which Thucydides describes how the reprieve was effected (a particularly good example of Thucydides "doing" tension and suspense). A ship had already been sent off to Mytilene to carry out the Assembly's original decision, and:

> . . . Immediately another trireme was sent out in all haste, since they feared that, unless it overtook the first trireme, they would find on their arrival that the city had been destroyed. The first trireme had a start of about twenty-four hours. The ambassadors from Mytilene provided wine and barley for the crew and promised great rewards if they arrived in time, and so the men made such speed on the voyage that they kept on rowing while they took their food . . . and rowed continually, taking it in turn to sleep. Luckily they had no wind against them, and as the first ship was not hurrying on its distasteful mission, while they were pressing on with such speed, what happened was that the first ship arrived so little ahead of them that Paches had just had time to read the decree and to prepare to put it into force, when the second ship put in to the harbour and prevented the massacre. So narrow had been the escape of Mytilene.
>
> *History of the Peloponnesian War* 3 49
> Translation: Rex Warner

The inhabitants of the island of Melos, later on in the war, were not so fortunate: for daring to attempt to remain neutral from Athens, they met the fate that Mytilene so narrowly avoided. Athens' much-vaunted freedom was not an ideal it shared with the victims of its aggression.

What this story also illustrates so vividly is that the single most important motor of Athenian democracy was the spoken word—rhetoric. What caused the change of heart, the sending forth of the second ship, was an emergency Assembly session, with speeches passionately representing each side of the question. It is not true to say that Athenian democracy caused the birth of political oratory, for even in Homer there are so many vivid examples of persuasive public speaking used to change the course of events for better or worse (think of Agamemnon's disastrous speech to his troops in the second book of the *Iliad*, or Telemachus' speech to the Ithacan Assembly in Book 2 of the *Odyssey*). But it is certainly true to say that Athenian democracy caused rhetoric to flower and to develop into an art: indeed it is no exaggeration to say that in Athens politics *was* public speaking. In a system lacking political parties, or specialist ministers holding recognized office, any Athenian citizen could speak up in the Assembly, and directly affect matters of state.

Achieving political power, then, was absolutely dependent upon a citizen's ability to speak persuasively. Expensive teachers known as sophists sprang up to train ambitious, wealthy young men in the subtle craft of rhetoric (among other subjects). Rhetoric continued to be a crucial part of ancient and medieval education; and one of the great inheritors of the ancient rhetorical tradition—since medieval education and the church were inextricably linked—is Christian preaching, especially in its vivid modern manifestation in the US. But of course the tradition is also alive in modern political discourse. The great speeches of antiquity, studied by generations of traditionally educated politicians, have echoed down the millennia (the

Gettysburg Address is, in some ways, a nineteenth-century version of Pericles' Funeral Oration). And today's politicians still use the tricks and turns of phrase that were classified and named by the ancient writers on rhetoric. Take the antimetabole. That, during the 2008 American presidential election, got itself a reputation as the campaigns' favorite rhetorical device. The most famous modern example of the trick—in which, in different parts of a sentence, word order is switched for maximum impact and a pleasing symmetry—was in John F. Kennedy's 1961 inauguration speech: "Ask not what your country can do for you—ask what you can do for your country." John McCain, on the campaign trail in 2008, used it thus: "We were elected to change Washington, and we let Washington change us."

Another device—a particular favorite of Barack Obama, whose election campaign saw him praised as a great orator in the ancient tradition—is the anaphora, which involves repeating the same words at the start of sentences. This is how he employed it in his election night victory speech of November 4, 2008: "It's the answer told by lines that stretched around schools and churches in numbers this nation has never seen . . . It's the answer spoken by young and old, rich and poor . . . It's the answer that led those who have been told for so long by so many to be cynical . . . to put their hands on the arc of history . . ." A close relation is epiphora—which is repeating a phrase at the end of sentences. He used this one in the same speech, closing paragraphs with the words "yes we can" no fewer than seven times. For Obama, these devices contributed to the sense of rhythm and musicality in his delivery—delivery being another matter of enormous importance in ancient Athens, with the most celebrated speaker of them all, Demosthenes, reputedly arguing that the three most important things in oratory were delivery, delivery, and delivery.

Of course, words are not deeds. As Hillary Clinton noted in the 2008 US election campaign (using the device of antimetabole, as it happens): "In the end the true test is not the speeches a president delivers, it's whether the president delivers on the speeches." She was niggling at a persistent criticism of Obama at the time: that his winning way with words would not necessarily translate into heft as a leader. She was tapping into a suspicion of slick political rhetoric almost as old as rhetoric itself. The Athenians were acutely aware of the dangers of persuasive speakers whipping up a crowd into a frenzy and manipulating the people for cynical ends—of demagoguery. The sophists who flocked to Athens in the fifth century were frequently controversial figures, pilloried and satirized by, for example, Aristophanes in his play *Clouds*, which portrays Socrates as a sharp-talking charlatan, turning young heads with his fancy ideas. Plato—who was at pains to claim that Socrates was not a sophist—marshals a host of arguments against rhetoric in his dialogue *Gorgias*, in which he has Socrates put forth the view that rhetoric is not an art, just a form of flattery used to manipulate the masses. Above all, after the oligarchic revolutions at the end of the fifth century, which briefly toppled democracy, sophists were regarded as having influenced the young, privileged men who fomented the coups (see chapter 8).

So much for the politics of the *polis*. But man does not live by laws alone. How else did this citizen body operate? Religious life was absolutely crucial in reinforcing the unity of the community. Athens was studded with temples and sanctuaries, not just to the major "Olympian" gods, but to deities ranging from immortalized heroes to the north wind. Local demes had their own cults, as did Cleisthenes' "tribes." Worship of the gods revolved around sacrifice: an animal would be led in procession by the priest and attendants, have water dribbled on its head, and then be ritually slaughtered, with a libation of wine sprinkled too. The year was marked by innumerable festivals of civic and religious significance. The most famous of these were the City Dionysia and the Panathenaea, where representatives of all of Athens (even women, children, slaves, and foreigners) processed to the Parthenon and dedicated a robe to Athens' patron goddess, Athena Polias. The City Dionysia was the festival of Dionysus at which the great tragedies of Aeschylus, Sophocles, and Euripides were performed. Each of the three performance days would see productions of a tragic trilogy and a satyr play by a single playwright. (The satyr plays, of which only one complete example, Euripides' *Cyclops*, survives, seem characteristically to have involved the sort of heroic characters who appeared in tragedies alongside a chorus of satyrs. These were unruly, mischievous, lusty wild men with horses' ears and tails and goats' legs, part of the god Dionysus' traditional retinue.)

The plays' chorus costs would be covered by a *choregos*, a wealthy citizen appointed by one of the archons. The actors would be paid by the state. On the fourth performance day, five comedies would be staged, and the final day saw the judges, ordinary citizens chosen by lot, award the winning playwright a wreath of ivy. Lest we confuse it with a sort of ancient Stratford-upon-Avon, it is worth pointing out that before the plays got under way, there were two days of processions and sacrifices. The sons of citizens killed in war were paraded in full armor, and at the height of the empire, tribute from her allies was also displayed. And, unlike theater in modern-day times, plays were not a minority interest. Informed guesswork suggests that the theater that stood on the slopes of the Acropolis in the fifth century could seat 14,000; the citizen body, by way of a reminder, numbered about 30,000. There is even some (disputed) evidence that poorer citizens may have been compensated for loss of earnings while attending the plays (only think of that!). Sheer bums on seats vastly outstrip anything we are used to: the largest purpose-built theater in London, for instance, is the Coliseum, home of English National Opera, and it seats 2,374.

THE ORESTEIA

Aeschylus' *Oresteia*, first produced in 458, is the only trilogy of ancient Greek tragedies that survives in its entirety. Like many Greek dramas, the story of the first play, *Agamemnon*, springs directly from Homer. In Argos, a watchman on the city walls sights the beacon that means that Agamemnon is on his way home from the Trojan War (the watchman is a detail mentioned in *Odyssey* Book 4, when Menelaus is telling Telemachus the story of Agamemnon's return from Troy). Agamemnon arrives, with the captive Trojan princess Cassandra in his entourage. Clytemnestra, Agamemnon's wife, gives her husband an over-the-top welcome, persuading him to step upon the gorgeously rich purple cloth she lays before him—a temptation that he initially resists but to which he eventually succumbs. In the play this is a symbolic gesture of huge importance: his arrogance is made unnervingly physical, and the purple cloth—which resembles a tide of blood—foreshadows the slaughter that's to come. Agamemnon goes inside the house with his wife. Cassandra, who has the gift of prophecy (but the curse that no one will take her seriously) accurately foretells Agamemnon's doom. Sure enough, Clytemnestra soon emerges, followed by her lover Aegisthus, having murdered Agamemnon.

The second play is called *Choephoroi* ("libation bearers"). The play opens as Electra, daughter of Clytemnestra and Agamemnon, appears at her father's tomb accompanied by a group of foreign slave-women, the chorus of libation bearers. There she is met by her long-absent brother Orestes, who has returned from exile to take his revenge on his mother and her lover. He kills Aegisthus first and then, after a heartstopping encounter with his mother, slays her too. The third play, *Eumenides*, sees Orestes hounded by the Furies, the primeval deities who punish kindred-murder. At Delphi, the god Apollo promises to help Orestes, and the scene moves to Athens, where a sort of courtroom drama ensues, with Orestes' homicide case tried before Athena on the Areopagus hill and with Apollo speaking in support of the defendant. The jury is split evenly, but Athena's casting vote acquits Orestes. The Furies are transformed into Eumenides, "kindly ones."

The trilogy has been read as charting man's ascent from a primitive past of unendable blood-feuds and tit-for-tat "justice" toward a more rational present where the rule of law obtains; it also appears to be a case where an ostensibly mythic drama referred more or less explicitly to contemporary Athenian issues. Ephialtes' reforms in 462/1 had reconfigured the Areopagus' powers so that its main function was to operate as a homicide court, a move to which *Eumenides* surely alludes, giving its modern manifestation an origin deeply rooted in the past.

For the modern visitor to Athens, it is the Acropolis in general, and the Parthenon in particular, that is the most potent living traces of the *polis* of ancient Athens. The ruins of the Parthenon still bring out all kinds of emotional responses in us: wonder at the longevity of this bright marble; romantic fancy at the "aura" of the antique; admiration at the sheer ingenuity and beauty of the architecture; dismay, perhaps even, at the dispersal of the famous decorations from the Parthenon to museums around Europe. The most notorious example of this dispersal is the case of the Parthenon frieze, half of which Lord Elgin, the Fife-born aristocrat and British ambassador to the Ottoman Empire from 1799 to 1803, dislodged from its original position and shipped to England, where it can now be seen in the British Museum, part of the collection of sculptures known as the "Elgin Marbles." It was an act that was wildly controversial from the outset, and remains a live political issue to this day.

The buildings of the Acropolis—including the Parthenon, the temple of Athena Nike ("victory"), and the exquisite Erechtheum with its famous row of caryatids (sculpted female figures which take the place of columns)—were brought into existence in the aftermath of the Persian Wars. Persian troops had torched the Acropolis and its existing religious buildings not once but twice during the conflict, in 480 and 479. Nothing was left there but smouldering ruins, and it stayed a mess for a generation after the Persians were finally routed later in 479.

Under Pericles, however, an ambitious building program was begun. Like many major state building projects to this day, it did not go off without a hitch (the architectural master-planner, the famous sculptor Phidias, was accused of siphoning off money and procuring young ladies for Pericles on their site visits). But Plutarch, admittedly writing when the buildings were already 500 years old, remarked on how quickly they had been completed. Work was begun on the Parthenon in 447 and finished in 432.

Then and now, the visitor would approach the Acropolis via the Propylaea, a gate with Doric columns almost as elaborate as a temple. To the left was an art gallery hung with paintings that we can only dream about (Greek painting was praised to the skies in antiquity, but painted wood panels being less durable than bronze, marble, and ceramics, there is nothing to see now). As the visitor walked through the Propylaea, he or she would be greeted with a view of the northwest corner of the Parthenon; the temple was seen to its best advantage at an angle, so you could take in the extraordinary, seventy-meter length of its lateral colonnade and the effect of the splendid polychrome (for it was not dazzling white as we see it now, but elaborately painted). It is just under twice as long as it is wide: the ratio is 9:4, which is also the ratio between its width and its height (excluding the pediment). There is also a particularly extraordinary refinement at play: none of the columns is exactly vertical, but all lean inwards, such that (it has been calculated) they would meet at a central position about a mile above the roof of the temple were they continued at their existing angle. This prevents the eye from reading the columns as leaning outwards slightly when the building is seen from below. The front of the temple was in fact at its east end, so you would take in much of the exterior before reaching the entrance. You would, for example, see the decoration on both pediments; at the west end the carvings depicted the contest between Athena and Poseidon for the patronage of Athens (he offered a pool of water, she successfully proffered an olive tree). The east pediment, now in the British Museum, showed the miraculous birth of Athena as she sprang fully armed from the head of Zeus. The visitor would also have perhaps glanced upwards at the metopes, the panels above the columns and below the pediments, which were carved with mythological battle scenes: Amazons versus Athenians, gods versus giants.

If the visitor was feeling particularly curious, he or she might also have strained for a sight of the carved frieze above the inner row of pillars, half of which now resides in the British Museum: a master-piece of fluid, detailed, beautifully composed sculpture. Running in a 160-meter-long ribbon around the building (120 meters or so survives intact), it depicts a procession, with horses and sacrificial animals, culminating in a rather baffling scene involving a child, a man, some women, the gods, and a piece of cloth. In the eighteenth century it was proposed that the frieze referred to the Panathenaea, the annual religious festival in which a new robe was dedicated to Athena. This is a clever conjecture, but no one has come up with a completely satisfying explanation for the scenes on the frieze.

Quite possibly, however, the visitor wouldn't really notice the Parthenon frieze, or wouldn't pause to study it. There was a lot more to see and Pausanias, the first author to produce a guidebook entry to the Parthenon, in the second century AD, didn't even mention it. He was gearing up for the main event: when you walked through the door of the temple you would be punched in the face by the sight of the (now lost) statue of Athena Parthenos inside. She was a stag-gering ten meters tall. Her flesh was ivory, her breastplate gold, her eyes gems. To be honest, she sounds rather horrible, or at least rather frightening. You wouldn't want to mess with her, this spear-wielding, helmeted protector of Athens. The *polis* may have consisted of the people: but nothing could be a more downright assertion of Athens' domineering power than the Parthenon.

For me, the Parthenon is like a synecdoche for Athens' democracy: it was (and is) enviable, dazzling, elegant, much copied, ahead of its time—and yet there was something troubling about this don't-mess-with-me symbol of power and glory. We idealize Athenian democracy, and yet it only became an ideal: it began as a pragmatic solution to political strife, and as it went on, wealthy men from aristocratic families (like Pericles) sought and gained power, and were successfully elected year after year to its most influential posts. Egalitarianism was not the end of the story. That's not to deny that Athenian democracy bracingly did away with political distinctions between rich and poor, and was crucial in developing important ideas about citizenship. Nor can one fail to be moved by Pericles' funeral oration when he enjoins the Athenians to "fall in love" with their city, and when he talks about the engaged relationship between man and *polis*:

> Here each individual is interested not only in his own affairs but in the affairs of state as well: even those who are mostly occupied with their own business are extremely well-informed on general politics—this is a peculiarity of ours: we do not say that a man who takes no interest in politics is a man who minds his own business here at all. We Athenians, in our own persons, take our decisions on policy or submit them to proper discussions: for we do not think that there is an incompatibility between words and deeds; the worst thing is to rush into action before the consequences have been properly debated.
>
> *History of the Peloponnesian War* 2 40
> Translation: Rex Warner

If only, in these times of apparently increasing political apathy, we could make the same claims for our own citizenry. What a challenge Pericles sets down. And yet citizenship in Athens was an exclusive affair: only about 10 percent of the population took part in this power-of-the-people. The rhetoric of inclusion in Pericles' speech masks exclusion. Darker still, perhaps, was the fact that domestic equality and fairness (as far as it went) also masked brutality abroad. But, then again, maybe it should not surprise us in the twenty-first century that aggressive imperialism was present at the birth of the distant ancestor of our own modern democracies.

PERICLES

Think of Greek statesmen, and we think at once of Pericles, the great politician immortalized by Thucydides, particularly in his famous funeral oration commemorating the dead in the opening rounds of the Peloponnesian War, in which he sets forth Athens as the ideal *polis*, an "education to all Greece." (In fact, we have no idea how far, if at all, Thucydides' words reflect an actual speech.) Born in about 495, Pericles was part of the aristocratic clan Alcmaeonidae, of which Cleisthenes was also a scion. He was *choregos* (funder of the chorus) for Aeschylus' play *The Persians* in 472, and came to prominence through his part in the prosecution of the powerful general and politician Cimon; and through his reform of the homicide court, the Areopagus.

According to his first- to second-century AD biographer Plutarch, he became one of the most influential men in Athens after Cimon's eventual ostracism. He was in charge of Athens' public-building works in the 440s and 430s—a program that had the Parthenon at its heart. He was also responsible for bringing forward legislation limiting Athenian citizenship to those with two Athenian parents. From the mid-440s, he was elected general every year, becoming Athens' de facto leader, and pursuing an ambitious foreign policy that resulted in the outbreak of the conflict against Sparta known as the Peleponnesian War. Thucydides says that he had integrity and vision; and that he led the people rather than currying favor with them. He was unhappily married, and his mistress was the famous courtesan Aspasia. Pericles died of the plague that swept through Athens in 429.

ARCHITECTURE AND THE PARTHENON

The *DORIC* was the simplest of classical
architectural orders, with somewhat stocky,
fluted shafts, about four to six times as tall as
they were wide, and a simple top (capital)
cushioning the architrave and metopes. The
Parthenon was essentially a Doric temple,
with a scattering of Ionic features.

Utterly elegant, the *IONIC* column was taller
and skinnier than the Doric, with 24 flutes, and
topped by delicate whorled volutes (the same
word applies to the beautiful spirals of a
snail's shell).

For the sake of classical completeness, here
is the *CORINTHIAN*, though it was rarely
used in Greece, and is much more a feature
of Roman buildings, such as the Pantheon in
Rome. The capital is decorated with stylized
acanthus leaves.

THE PARTHENON

The great temple of Athena Parthenos in Athens is what is
known as a "peripteral" temple (the word derives from the
Greek for wing). That is, it had a ring of columns surrounding
its main body which consisted of a *naos* (inner sanctuary) and
porches. The temple was (and is) celebrated for the virtuosity
of its decorative sculptures. Those on its pediments showed the
birth of Athena (east side) and the dispute between Athena and
Poseidon for control of Athens (west side).

Beneath the pediments are the metopes, each 1.3 meters
square, which were decorated with scenes of mythical battles,
including Lapiths versus Centaurs; gods versus giants; and
Athenians versus Amazons. From the diagram overleaf one can
also see where the frieze of the Parthenon was—and how the

visitor would have seen it in chunks, so to speak, through the outer columns of the peristyle.

Plan of the Parthenon

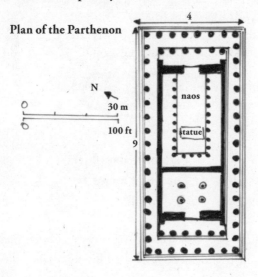

The position of the sculptures on the Parthenon

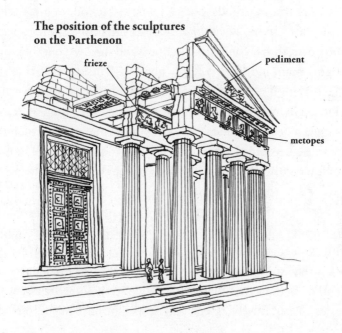

4. Pandora's daughters:
The silent majority

IT WAS FROM the very first throat-clearings of Greek literature that sprang our old friend, misogyny. In Hesiod's poem the *Theogony*, woman is made by Zeus as a punishment for men, after Prometheus steals fire from the gods. She is, remarks Hesiod, "a great affliction to mortals." In his *Works and Days*, it is that first woman, Pandora, who opens the jar containing sickness and sorrows: out they all pour, to sting mankind for ever. Only hope stays inside, caught under the lid. In Hesiod's world—where men must struggle against nature to scratch a living from the soil—woman is at best a drag on resources, the queen bee the drones must keep in the manner to which she has become accustomed. At worst, she's out to fleece you. "Do not let a woman poking into your barn deceive your mind by showing off her arse," warns the poet.

Fortunately, Homer's women are a delight. Admittedly, the *Iliad* is very largely about men; though the plot is fueled by problems with women. (Helen, whose abduction is the cause of the Trojan War itself; and Briseis, whose forced removal by Agamemnon from Achilles is the cause of the latter's wrath.) Nonetheless, the goddesses Thetis, Athena, Hera, and Aphrodite have major roles to play;

and Andromache, Hector's wife, stars in two of the most affecting scenes in the poem (see chapter 9). When the goddesses appear in the *Iliad*, in their less martial moments it can mean a pretty startling change of mood. In Book 14, after a very long, rather overwhelming bout of spears and arrows and death, we get some very *soigné* Hollywood glamor as we are shown Hera, in all her Gloria Swanson–ish gorgeousness, at her dressing table. She is making herself ready to seduce her husband, Zeus; her plan is to have her way in the fighting for a bit while he has a postcoital snooze. Here she is in her boudoir:

> She slipped in, closing the polished doors behind her.
> The ambrosia first. Hera cleansed her enticing body
> of any blemish, then she applied a deep olive rub,
> the breath-taking, redolent oil she kept beside her . . .
> one stir of the scent in the bronze-floored halls of Zeus
> and a perfumed cloud would drift from heaven down to earth.
> Kneading her skin with this to a soft glow and combing her
> > hair,
> she twisted her braids with expert hands, and sleek, luxurious,
> shining down from her deathless head they fell, cascading.
> > *Iliad* 14 208–213

Gosh, even I am overwhelmed by Hera's femininity here.

There are similar mood changes afoot when mortal women—self-possessed queens and princesses a world away from the peasant society conjured by Hesiod—play their part in the *Iliad*. Admittedly, we don't get to hear very much about Briseis (we are told she wept when she was taken away from Achilles, and that's about it). But the Trojan women are a bit different. With Andromache, we get a sense of what the home side are fighting for. With Helen, we get a sense of what they are fighting over. Is she worth it? Well, she herself says she wishes she'd died long since and prevented all these ghastly years of bloodshed . . . and yet, when she sashays her way past the city's venerable old men in Book 3, as lovely as the girl from Ipanema, she causes a frisson:

> And catching sight of Helen moving along the ramparts,
> they murmured one to another, gentle, winged words:
> "Who on earth could blame them? Ah, no wonder
> the men of Troy and Argives under arms have suffered
> years of agony for her, for such a woman."
>
> *Iliad* 3 185–189

The half-admired, half-loathed Helen has something slightly otherworldly about her, a sense of detachment, of superior insight. In Book 3, we see her weaving a robe decorated with scenes from the war, "working into the weft the endless bloody struggles / stallion-breaking Trojans and Argives armed in bronze / had suffered all for her at the god of battle's hands." It's as if she already knows that the Trojan War will be a matter of future legend; she can see beyond the immediate . . . but then she is the child of Zeus. Aside from a few words from Priam, Helen's is the last voice we hear in the entire poem, as she mourns Hector—the hero who was, she says, her only ally, the only man who understood her. "Now there is no one left / in the wide realm of Troy, no friend to treat me kindly— / all the countrymen cringe from me in loathing." One can't help but feel sorry for her.

In the *Odyssey* we meet Helen again, and here she is very much the self-possessed hostess, more than equal, we feel, to any situation. She is installed once more as Menelaus' wife in Sparta when Telemachus arrives in search of news of his father, in Book 4. Menelaus, who does not come off as the sharpest knife in the block, has not worked out the identity of his young guest; but Helen gets it immediately: he looks exactly like his father, she says. As the couple and their guests weep at the memory of Troy and the misfortunes of Odysseus, Helen does something rather disturbing: she secretly drugs everyone's wine so that they forget the pain and suffering of the past. She is not a straightforward creature, this Helen, by any stretch of the imagination. But she is immensely perceptive, and she knows what she is about . . . if Telemachus is doubtful about whether he is truly the son of his father, and what that might mean, then her instant recognition of him must help awaken his maturing sense of self. And when Telemachus wants to know what his father was *really* like, she tells him, by providing a memory from the Trojan war of Odysseus at his most Odysseus-like: how he dressed himself in rags and slipped into Troy as a spy . . . unrecognized by everyone except, of course, Helen. Nothing gets past her.

The *Odyssey*, by contrast with the *Iliad*, is absolutely brimming with brilliant women characters, chief among them the magnificent Penelope herself. Margaret Atwood has written a "corrective" version of the *Odyssey* called the *Penelopiad*, told from Penelope's point of view; I admire Atwood enormously, but Penelope's presence is so strong in the *Odyssey* anyway that I feel one hardly needs this kind of thing. It is Penelope, after all, who gets the last laugh. She (apart from old Laertes) is the final character on Ithaca to whom Odysseus reveals himself. But there's absolutely no question of her taking him on trust. Instead, she tests him out, and gives the kind of grilling that suggests she's more than his equal in subterfuge and subtlety. Still unsure about his identity—or is she feinting?—after Odysseus presents himself to her as her husband, she coolly suggests that their bed be moved out of the bridal chamber and placed on the porch:

Putting her husband to the proof—but Odysseus
blazed up in fury, lashing out at his loyal wife:
"Woman—your words, they cut me to the core!
Who could move my bed? Impossible task,

71

even for some skilled craftsman—unless a god
came down in person, quick to lend a hand,
lifted it out with ease and moved it elsewhere.
Not a man on earth, not even at peak strength,
would find it easy to prise it up and shift it, no,
a great sign, a hallmark lies in its construction."

Odyssey 23 203–10

Odysseus explains how he made the bed himself; and no man can move it, because one of its posts was fashioned from the living, rooted trunk of an olive tree. Finally, joyfully, Penelope accepts him: not another soul, except for a single maid, knew the secret of the olive-tree bed. This is how the poet describes her outpouring of emotion:

Joy, warm as the joy that shipwrecked sailors feel
when they catch sight of land—Poseidon has struck
their well-rigged ship on the open sea with gale winds
and crushing walls of waves, and only a few escape, swimming,
struggling out of the frothing surf to reach the shore,
their bodies crusted with salt but buoyed up with joy
as they plant their feet on solid ground again,
spared a deadly fate. So joyous now to her
the sight of her husband, vivid in her gaze,
that her white arms, embracing his neck,
would never for a moment let him go . . .

Odyssey 23 262–72

What I love about this simile is that it puts Penelope's experience on a par with Odysseus'. She is likened to that shipwrecked, salt-caked sailor who *he* has so often been . . .

Circe, who turns her gentlemen callers into pigs; Nausicaa, the charming ingenue, princess of Phaeacia, who has a beadily perceptive way with her: these dames are a hoot, and I must say I particularly enjoy Calypso's proto-feminist outburst to Hermes when she is told she can't keep Odysseus any longer: "You male gods, the only reason you don't like goddesses sleeping with men is that you're jealous." (I paraphrase, but this is the spirit.) In fact, so very richly drawn are the women of the *Odyssey* that more than one reader has been moved to suggest that the poem must have been written by a woman: and by no one is this theory more hilariously put forward than by Samuel Butler, author of *The Way of All Flesh*, in his often insightful, deeply batty book *The Authoress of the Odyssey* (1897).

For Butler, there was no greater delight on earth than to prove an irritation to the academy and the establishment. *The Authoress* is more of an extended provocation than a work of scholarship—though Butler was no mean classicist, having studied at school under the very Benjamin Kennedy who wrote *Kennedy's Shorter Latin Primer*; and later at St. John's College, Cambridge. But *The Authoress* is a terrific read, and along its utterly bonkers way contains some fascinating observations. It is certainly not what you'd call a feminist work: to argue that the author of the poem must have been a woman because, for example, the poet is strikingly concerned with domestic minutiae (like the mopping-down of Odysseus' dining hall after the suitors' slaughter) is not perhaps a position that would have Germaine Greer cheering from the sidelines. Only a woman could have created such dominating, assertive women characters, argues Butler; and only a woman could have created such drippy men. (In this he likens the "authoress" of the *Odyssey* to Jane Austen.) He also points out various "mistakes," that, in his view, a male writer couldn't possibly have made. No man, for instance, would have given Odysseus' boat (the one he makes on Calypso's island) two rudders: "Probably the writer of the *Odyssey* forgot for the moment at which end the rudder should be" he offers. "She thought it all over yesterday, and was not going to think it all over again today, so she put the rudder at

73

both ends, intending to remove it from the one that should prove to be the wrong one; later on she forgot, or did not think it worthwhile to trouble about so small a detail."

My favorite part of the book, though, is when Butler asserts that the author is whitewashing Penelope: that the writer must be suppressing an older version of the story in which the heroine is anything but a paragon of virtue. He sees traces of this palimpsest in Penelope's treatment of the suitors. Why doesn't she get rid of them sooner? he asks. "Not one of [the suitors] ever finds out that his case is hopeless and takes his leave; and thus matters drift on year after year—during all which time Penelope is not getting any younger." He reckons that she must like having them there, as a sop to her increasingly middle-aged vanity. Hilarious it is, but not entirely ridiculous; readers still puzzle over some of Penelope's motivations. There's a moment where she gussies up and displays herself alluringly to the suitors. What's she up to, if she's so fed up with them? On another occasion she dreams that an eagle kills her geese. The dream-eagle explicitly identifies itself as her husband, but she weeps for the geese nonetheless. Why? We are not told: Homer does not "do" inner life (not much, anyway—we do get the odd flashes from Odysseus' deep soul). By and large, characters are sketched out through what they say and do, not what they think and feel. His characters rage when they are angry, weep when they are unhappy, and speak their minds. There are no resonating psychological layers; Penelope is not Isabel Archer. But she is no less vivid and alive for that.

One of the least crazy things Butler points out in his book is that there were a number of fine women poets in ancient Greece. The best known and best loved by far is the lyric poet Sappho, born in Lesbos in the second half of the seventh century. Though later writers moralized and fantasized about Sappho's life, the only real evidence about her circumstances is contained within her work, the vast majority of which is fragmentary. Of her wonderful poems of love and longing, many are unambiguously homoerotic; some are wedding songs. Part of their appeal is their very fragmentary quality: these beautiful lines and half-lines are like finely decorated potsherds, separated forever from their fellows—they act as a poignant metaphor, perhaps, of the study of the ancient world itself, the way we try to make a world from beautiful scraps and bits. In fact there is a (part) poem of hers that was actually discovered written on a potsherd; fragment two, as it is known:

> down from the mountain top
> and out of Crete,
>   come to me here
> in your sacred precinct, to your grove
> of apple trees,
>   and your altars
>   smoking with incense,
> where cold water flows babbling
> through the branches,
>   the whole place
>   shadowed with roses,
>   sleep adrift down
> from silvery leaves
>   an enchantment
>
> horses grazing in a meadow
>   abloom with spring flowers
> and where the breezes blow sweetly,
>
>
>   here, Cypris,
> delicately in golden cups
>   pour nectar
>   mixed for our festivities.

Translation: Stanley Lombardo

It is an invocation, a summoning of the goddess Aphrodite, named here for Cyprus, the island off which she was born from the foam of the sea. It's astonishingly powerful, this evocation of place, an apple grove in which the love goddess's sanctuary lies. It's synaesthetic, almost every sense is stimulated: there's the heady scent of the incense; the sight of the stream (in the background) with the shading apple trees in front; the icy coldness of the water; the drowsy sound of the breeze through the leaves; beyond, the glimpse of the horses grazing in the flower-filled meadows. To read this poem is to be there, lying in the deep grass of the grove, gently heading for sleep . . .

Fifth-century Athens, however, was a very different place from the aristocratic world of seventh-century Lesbos, and indeed from the even earlier world that echoes through the poems of Homer. Athens at the height of its intellectual revolution, when it was bringing forth the Parthenon, the beginnings of science, the great tragedies, history, rhetoric, philosophy, and a host of other marvels, was also extraordinarily and uncomfortably repressive to its women. In Pericles' funeral oration in Thucydides' *History of the Peloponnesian War*, the statesman talks long and stirringly about those who have died for their city, and what Athens stands for: freedom, tolerance, and equality before the law, no matter what a citizen's means. Finally, in the last paragraph of that great speech, he gets to the women:

> Perhaps I should say a word or two on the duties of women to those among you who are now widowed. I can say all I have to say in a short word of advice. Your great glory is not to be inferior to what god has made you, and the greatest glory of a woman is to be least talked about by men, whether they are praising you or criticising you.

History of the Peloponnesian War 2 46
Translation: Rex Warner

76

This was all very different from the life of Spartan girls, who, unusually, were given an education and training in athletics. Scandalously (to other Greeks), they were to be seen exercising wearing short dresses, a breast exposed. When they were married, their husbands lived communally in barracks, visiting their wives by night, surreptitiously and rarely. Spartan women could inherit property; and one Spartan woman was even a reputed horse trainer. One Cynisca trained a team that triumphed in the Olympic Games chariot races of 396 and 392. She erected a monument, with a still-visible, utterly remarkable inscription that reads:

> My fathers and brothers were Spartan kings,
> I won with a team of fast-footed horses,
> and put up this monument: I am Cynisca:
> I say I am the only woman in all Greece
> to have won this wreath.

Simone de Beauvoir wrote appreciatively of the Spartan system in *The Second Sex*:

> If a society that forbids private property also rejects the family, the lot of women in it is found to be considerably ameliorated. In Sparta the communal regime was in force, and it was the only Greek city in which woman was treated almost on an equality with men.

I think de Beauvoir is rather overexcited here: the primary function of Spartan women seems to have been to produce healthy Spartan warriors, all very Germany-before-the-war, frankly. Still, Spartan women were apparently quite exceptional, though we know about them very largely from hostile Athenian, rather than Spartan, sources. A couple of stories about the Spartan woman Gorgo in Herodotus illustrate the point. First, as an eight-year-old girl, she is ordered by her father, King Cleomenes, to sit in on a meeting between him and Aristagoras, the tyrant of Miletus in Ionia, modern Turkey. Aristagoras was trying to get Spartan support against the Persians, and offered Cleomenes a financial sweetener (as well as pointing out that since the Persians were effeminate trouser-wearers, they *must* be easy to beat). But Gorgo piped up that Aristagoras, with his brown envelopes, was a corrupting influence, an intervention with which her father was very pleased. Later, in adult life (again, according to Herodotus), when she was married to the soon-to-be war hero Leonidas, the Spartans received a puzzling letter: a wax tablet with absolutely nothing written on it. Gorgo had the bright idea of scraping off the wax and, lo and behold, scratched into the wood beneath was a letter from the Spartan exile Demaratus—warning his former friends, with a little of his old Spartan loyalty intact, that his new best friend, Xerxes of Persia, was planning to invade Greece. By repute, when a foreign traveler said to Gorgo on one occasion, "You Laconian women are the only ones who can rule men," she replied, "That is because we are the only ones who give birth to (real) men." (Laconia was the region around Sparta.) The gist of that aperçu, which is collected in Plutarch's book *Spartan Sayings*, is given to the actress Lena Headey in the film *300*, Zak Snyder's vividly stylized account of the battle of Thermopylae. In fact, Plutarch records quite a few terse witticisms from the mouths of Spartan women. Argileonis, mother of the general Brasidas, a hero of the Peloponnesian War, is supposed to have sent him off to battle with the words "Come back with your shield—or on it," a line cleverly pinched and also given to Gorgo in *300*.

A well-off, respectable Athenian woman, by contrast, might not even speak to passersby in the street, or open her own front door . . . she was to be seeing to household tasks: cooking, wool-working, and child-rearing. Officially, Athenian women could inherit property. In reality, however, if that happened they were likely to be claimed in marriage by their nearest available male relative, who would simply take control of the inheritance. Not that every woman in Athens was either well off or respectable, of course. The poorer Athenian citizen wives might have worked in the shops in the *agora*, the marketplace. Of course, there were plenty of prostitutes, slaves mostly, whom you could find in Athens' Ceramicus district, just by the Dipylon gate, and there was, too, the perfumed, rarefied breed of courtesan called *hetaira*, which means companion. A far cry from common tarts, these courtesans were elegant, sophisticated creatures whose status as "paid-for" was hushed up in a courtly, dignified game of present-buying and favor-giving. In the fourth century, the great sculptor Praxiteles was supposed to have made a statue of Love for his favorite squeeze Phryne, a marvelous masterpiece which she placed in the temple of Eros in Thespiae. Phryne also modeled for the sculptor, and was so rich she offered to pay for the walls of the city of Thebes to be rebuilt after Alexander the Great razed them. Pericles, famously, was the partner of the *hetaira* Aspasia, and she was pilloried on the comic stage for her supposed influence over the politician: in Aristophanes' comedy *Acharnians*, she gets to be responsible for the Peloponnesian War itself. In the play (produced in 425, safely after Pericles' death), the hero Dicaeopolis claims that the statesman was so obsessed by her that he made war on Sparta simply to retrieve two prostitutes who had strayed from her whorehouse. Plutarch's biography of Pericles claimed: "Aspasia was highly valued by Pericles because she was clever and politically astute."

Where women had an important role outside the home in Athens, leaving aside those who worked in the sex trade, was in religious ceremony—and in the theater. There were a number of women-only annual religious festivals, such as the Thesmophoria, in which married females spent three days living in Demeter's sanctuary near the Pnyx, the hill west of the Acropolis. In this autumn fertility rite, the celebrants probably mimicked the mourning of the goddess

Demeter for her daughter Persephone, who was abducted by Hades. (According to myth, Hades had tricked the kidnapped Persephone into eating some pomegranate seeds in the Underworld—and once you'd dined in the Underworld, that was it, there was no going back. But Demeter was so traumatized by her loss that the earth ceased to produce, so Zeus had to intervene and bend the rules to effect a compromise. In the end, Persephone spent part of the year with Hades in the Underworld, and part of it with her mother. While Demeter mourns her daughter's absence, winter falls on the earth; and when mother and daughter are reunited, summer reigns.)

When I say that women were visible in the theater, I mean that they were visible on the stage: in itself an illusion, since female parts were invariably played by men, and their roles invariably written by men. Nonetheless, the great Greek tragedies are bursting with larger-than-life women characters of quite astonishing vividness. Whether there were women in the *audience* for the great Athenian drama festivals remains a moot point. The evidence, such as it is, seems inconclusive, but it is a question that gets classicists really quite hot under the collar. Personally, for what it's worth, I think the answer is that there weren't, or at least not many (it seems possible there were a few priestesses who got to see the great works of Aeschylus, Sophocles, and Euripides).

One of the striking things about the subject matter of the vast bulk of Athenian tragedy was its sheer distance from the everyday. Here was the audience, living in their modern, radical democracy; and here were the tragedies, which, with some very few exceptions, were set in the long ago and the far away. Kings, gods, and heroes stalked the Athenian stage . . . not that these plays ignored the political and social realities of the contemporary *polis*, but they filtered them through these old stories. It is still true, of course, that sometimes the things that are closest to home can be most subtly treated at arm's length—which is perhaps why some of the most eloquent theatrical comments on contemporary warfare, have come from stagings of Greek drama, some of which contain veiled comments on the foreign policy of Athens at the time they were written.

These stories of far away and long ago were full of women: women who spoke out, did things, did not stay in the female quarters weaving. Take Aeschylus' Clytemnestra, for instance: in the *Oresteia* (see page 59) she gives her husband Agamemnon a fulsome welcome home from the Trojan War. But with her lover Aegisthus, she has plotted his death, a revenge for his slaughtering their daughter Iphigenia at the altar to ensure a fair wind as he and his men set out for Troy at the beginning of the war. In many ways, Clytemnestra was the archetypal monstrous woman for the Greeks, positioned in the *Odyssey* as the opposite of the loyal Penelope. But in the play she is also a great character, terrifying, powerful, given some of the most darkly poetic lines of this deeply disturbing and rich drama. But how was such a character "read" by contemporary audiences? one wonders. Were creatures like Clytemnestra bogeywomen, there to give the Athenian male citizenry nightmares? Or was there more to it than that? After all, Clytemnestra is not a wholly unsympathetic character; her actions are at least pyschologically plausible.

Sophocles' Antigone is another puzzling case in point. She is the daughter of Oedipus, now in exile after his terrible discovery that he has killed his father and married his mother (see chapter 2). Her uncle Creon is now king of Thebes. She has two brothers, Eteocles and Polynices. Eteocles remained loyal to the city, but Polynices raised an army and attacked it. The two brothers killed each other in battle. Creon decrees that Polynices, the traitor, must not be given proper burial rites (a big deal), but Antigone defies his decree and does so anyway. Her offense is punished by death, despite the pleas of Haemon, Creon's son and Antigone's fiancé. Finally Tiresias, the prophet, appears and reveals it was the gods' will to bury Polynices, but Creon is too late to effect a reprieve. Antigone is dead; Haemon is dead; and for good measure, Creon's wife kills herself too. He is left a broken man.

What's going on here? A casual going-over of the play suggests that Antigone is unambiguously in the right, and that is certainly how the case has been seen by many readers. The individual makes a stand against repressive authority, is martyred, and her position is vindicated: this all makes sense to us, and this is how Antigone has been played in, say, occupied France during the Second World War (in Jean Anouilh's version of the story). But others have also stressed the extent to which Creon stands for authority in a good way—for the *polis* as the focus of loyalty. Take Pericles' funeral oration in Thucydides: he urges his audience to "fall in love with" Athens; and he does not name a single one of the war dead whom his speech commemorates. In this ideology, it is the collective's devotion to the *polis* that matters, not the deeds or desires of the individual.

Then take *Medea* by Euripides. The setting is Corinth. Jason has returned from Colchis on the Black Sea, from where he snatched the Golden Fleece, with the help of the princess Medea. She fell in love with him and they married; they now have two sons. But Jason has abandoned her, and now married Glauce, daughter of the king of Corinth. Medea is furious. Her first speech, addressed to the chorus of Corinthian women, contains the following lines:

> Surely, of all creatures that have life and will, we women
> Are the most wretched. When, for an extravagant sum,
> We have bought a husband, we must then accept him as
> Possessor of our body. This is to aggravate
> Wrong with worse wrong. Then the great question: will
>   the man
> We get be bad or good? For women, divorce is not
> Respectable; to repel the man, not possible.
> Still more, a foreign woman, coming among new laws,

New customs, needs the skill of magic, to find out
What her home could not teach her, how to treat the man
Whose bed she shares. And if in this exacting toil
We are successful, and our husband does not struggle
Under the marriage yoke, our life is enviable.
Otherwise, death is better. If a man grows tired
Of the company at home, he can go out, and find
A cure for tediousness. We wives are forced to look
To one man only. And, they tell us, we at home
Live free from danger, they go out to battle: fools!
I'd rather stand three times in the front line than bear
One child.

Medea 230–251
Translation: Philip Vellacott

Go sister! (one is tempted to cry). It is hard not to read into this a commentary on the lives of real women in Euripides' contemporary Athens. But Medea really does turn out to be monstrous, the very archetype of the male fantasy of the bunny boiler. Using her sinister magical skills, she murders Glauce with a poisoned robe and a crown; and she kills her sons by Jason to punish him. Then she ascends, rather magnificently, in the chariot of the sun-god Helios, her grandfather, and takes off to seek sanctuary in . . . Athens, puzzlingly enough.

Euripides plays on fears of women's power and sexuality in *The Bacchae*, too. In this drama, Dionysus comes to Thebes to establish his cult in his own birthplace (he is the son of Zeus and Semele, princess of Thebes). With him he brings an entourage of foreign women, the "maenads" or "bacchantes" who are his worshippers and make up the play's chorus: sometimes they are gentle and pacific, though when they are celebrating their women-only orgiastic rites they might catch wild animals and rip them apart with their bare hands . . .

But the people of Thebes are resistant to the new cult: Pentheus, the king, denies the existence of the god, as do Semele's own sisters, one of whom, Agave, is Pentheus' mother. Dionysus is a gripping character, all silky deadliness and sleek sexual ambiguity. His revenge on those who deny him is total. In a wonderful and troubling scene, the god plays on Pentheus' prurience and repressed sexual curiosity, persuading him to dress as a woman to spy on the bacchanalian rites, which Pentheus' mother has now joined as a celebrant. A dazed Pentheus, dressed in drag, is led up to Mount Cithaeron to watch the ritual. But he returns dead: his mother, in a fit of unknowing, orgiastic ecstasy, has mistaken him for an animal and ripped his head from his shoulders.

There were real bacchantes, too, in classical Greece; every other year groups of women went off into the mountains to worship the god; maybe the men did rather wonder what they got up to when they were all alone. (Donna Tartt's novel *The Secret History*, in which a group of American classics students re-create Bacchic rites with disastrous consequences, is well worth the read, by the way.)

Real Athenian women are, for the most part, silent to us, refusing to allow themselves to be talked about, as Thucydides/ Pericles ordains. It is left to Herodotus to give voice to an entertaining cast of female characters (though none of his shrewd, clever women is Athenian). There is the unnamed wife of Candaules, king of Lydia: he made one of his henchmen spy on her naked, and her vengeance for this indignity had far-reaching consequences for the Lydian empire. (This is the story that Kristin Scott Thomas relates, as Katharine, in Anthony Minghella's film of *The English Patient*, see chapter 6.) There is Tomyris, the warlike queen of the uncivilized Massagetae tribe, who, having defeated the great Persian king, Cyrus, grotesquely plunged his corpse's head into a wineskin filled with blood. (In *Henry VI*, when the Countess of Auvergne hatches a plot to kill the mighty warrior Talbot, she says: "The plot is laid: if all things fall out right, / I shall as famous be by this exploit / As Scythian Tomyris by Cyrus' death.") There is Phaedymia, who identifies King Cambyses of Persia's successor, Smerdis, as an imposter (by surreptitiously feeling around his head as he slept; the clue was that the imposter had no ears). It is Atossa, the wife of King Darius of Persia, who, in bed with him one night, advises him to turn his imperial ambitions towards Greece. ("I have heard what good servants Laconian, Argive, Attic, and Corinthian girls make, and I'd love to have some," she says. You can feel delicious chills of horror running down the spines of Herodotus' Greek audience.) And then there is Artemisia, the Persian ally and queen of the Greek city of Halicarnassus (Herodotus' own birthplace, now the Turkish resort of Bodrum). Not only does she give a very great deal of sensible tactical advice to Xerxes of Persia during his attempted invasion of Greece (which he ignores), but she also becomes the only leader on the Persian side to emerge from the battle of Salamis as a war hero: at least that's what Xerxes thinks. During the battle, the ship she is commanding is pursued by an Athenian vessel. Her path forward blocked, she turns about and rams a friendly ship. The Athenian boat assumes she's a Greek ally after all, and turns away; the ship she'd rammed sinks, all hands lost. Xerxes sees all this and is deeply impressed—because he assumes that the rammed ship was an enemy vessel. And luckily for her, no one from it remains alive to put him right. According to Herodotus, Xerxes exclaimed: "My men have turned into women and my women into men."

As one of the few historical occasions in which a fifth-century woman (albeit one on the "wrong" side) gets one up on a man, it is, frankly, an episode to relish. Despite being silenced, hidden, and feared, Greek women couldn't entirely be blotted out into invisibility. Even as they emerge from the imaginations and fantasies of men, we can still enjoy these towers of resourcefulness, intelligence, and strength. If Odysseus is the epitome of bright-eyed shrewdness and canny sagacity, then Penelope is more than a match for him. And I'd love to see that hero of fiction even try to outwit those real queens, the formidable Gorgo, the warlike Tomyris, or, best of all, the serenely amoral, wily Artemisia.

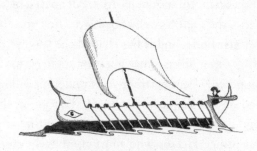

5. Swords and sandals:
War in Homer, Herodotus, and Thucydides

Homer's war

T. E. LAWRENCE WAS fond enough of Homer to translate him (rather ploddingly), but that didn't stop him from pouring mild scorn on the poet's war-worthiness. Homer's battle scenes were all wrong, he thought. Homer must have been "very bookish" and "a house-bred man," unlike T. E., who had himself "hunted wild boars and watched wild lions"—animals to which Homer frequently compared his ravening fighters.

As countless scholars and readers have pointed out over the centuries, Homer's battles are, to say the least, stylized. Warriors have chariots, but oddly, they seem to use them only as conveyances to the battlefield. Soldiers invariably die instantly; like elegant Hollywood deaths, these exits are all far too neat. Within the chaos of the fray, combatants on opposite sides have the opportunity to swap what are, in practical terms, absurdly long speeches, not unlike the implausible battlefield encounters in Shakespeare's history plays. The heroes Diomedes and Glaucus, for example, talk for ages during the fighting in Book 6, Glaucus producing a detailed account of his family history. If you really start to interrogate precisely what's happening militarily in the *Iliad*, things do, it's true, fall apart a bit.

Nonetheless, the *Iliad*, as well as being the first great book, is also the first great war book, and it has shaped the way we think about military conflict ever since. That goes for soldiers, too: Alexander the Great supposedly slept with the *Iliad* under his pillow; and even now it is read on the literature course at West Point, the US military academy. For Elizabeth Samet, professor of literature there, it is the Trojan prince Hector who most completely exemplifies the "citizen soldier" the academy aims to produce. "His martial ambitions always seem to me bound up with the survival of the city and the culture he defends," she has written, deftly Americanizing the hero. And Jonathan Shay, a psychiatrist who was an adviser to the US army personnel chief in 2004–5, has likened Achilles' terrible grief and bloodlust after the death of Patroclus to the berserking fury experienced by real American soldiers in Vietnam. Shay's angle on Homer, in his book *Achilles in Vietnam: Combat Trauma and the Undoing of Character*, came as a surprise to many classicists, who have tended to see Achilles' rage as a purely literary conceit, rather than an emotionally plausible portrait of a "real" soldier.

Furthermore, what that "unrealistic" encounter between Glaucus and Diomedes really suggests is a deeply human idea: the cruel fact that two men who could be friends are caught up in battle against each other. Homer's heroes fight for personal glory and honor, for immortal fame, though their lives will be cut short. But despite that, some of them—notably Achilles—can offer a critique of the war. In Book 1, the hero points out that the Trojans have never done him any harm; it's only out of loyalty to Agamemnon that he's fighting at all—a sentiment that must have been echoed by weary troopers countless times down the millennia. The emptiness of the warrior's code is drawn out by Achilles in Book 9, when he gives his answer to the "embassy" sent by Agamemnon to urge him back to the battlefield:

> One and the same lot for the man who hangs back
> and the man who battles hard. The same honour waits
> for the coward and the brave. They both go down to Death,
> the fighter who shirks, the one who works to exhaustion.
>
> *Iliad* 9 385–388

But Homer (not to mention Achilles) is no peacenik. The combat between these soldiers is often bloody and grotesque—but just as often magnificent. One of the striking ways in which the poet illuminates the larger-than-life encounters of these heroic warriors (of whom today's men, he tells us, are mere shadows) is his technique of the extended simile. When Hector (or Diomedes or Ajax or whoever it might be) launches himself against a combatant, he is often likened to a powerful force from nature: a whirlwind, say, or a wild boar. At the end of Book 15, when Hector's power is gathering before it culminates in his butchering of Patroclus, he is, says Homer, like a lion making cattle stampede; or an eagle swooping down on flocks of birds. (It is a technique borrowed by the Homer-loving Philip Pullman in his book *The Golden Compass*, where he describes the unimaginable power of the two armored bears, Iofur and Iorek, as they clash in single combat: "Like two great masses of rock balanced on adjoining peaks and shaken loose by an earthquake, that bound down the mountainsides gathering speed . . .") Here's another, *echt*-Homeric example—Achilles has become the superhuman berserker, in the full flood of his rage after Patroclus' death, trapping a band of fleeing Trojans in the river Scamander, near to the city. Here, shockingly, he will show no mercy, but chokes the current with corpses so utterly and grotesquely that the river itself will later rise up in outrage to fight him:

Like shoals of fish darting before some big-bellied dolphin,
escaping, cramming the coves of a good deepwater harbour,
terrified for their lives—he devours all he catches—
so the Trojans down that terrible river's onrush
cowered under its bluffs.

Iliad 21 25–29

Achilles is like a dolphin hunting fish: this aquatic simile, perfect for its watery context, is unique in Homer.

It is just at this point that Achilles takes twelve young Trojans alive, ready to sacrifice them on the tomb of Patroclus, a human carnage that is horrific even in terms of the extremity of the *Iliad*. Indeed, Homer's descriptions as often make you wince as smile: there's a gruesome, cold-blooded sharpness to the way he will describe a spear or an arrow piercing the body just so (Patroclus in Book 16 hooks a Trojan, says Homer, on his spear like an angler hooking a fish). But there's also infinite pity, too, and sometimes an abundant beauty: a justly famous simile describes the death, by Teucer's arrow, of the Trojan Gorgythion:

As a garden poppy, burst into red bloom, bends,
drooping its head to one side, weighed down
by its full seeds and a sudden spring shower,
so Gorgythion's head fell limp over one shoulder,
weighed down by his helmet.

Iliad 8 349–353

One can't help speculating whether this passage took on a greater significance to fighters in the First World War, as the freshly disturbed sod of no-man's land threw up real scarlet poppies in the summer.

What I particularly love about the way Homer marshals similes in the *Iliad*, though, is that he uses them to summon up a humble, rural peacetime world, a world that is in abeyance, a world that is lost in the bloodlust of war. When Ajax is being slowly beaten back by the Trojans in Book 11, he's like a recalcitrant donkey that children are trying, with difficulty, to beat out of a cornfield. In the next book, the opposing armies fight like neighboring farmers scrapping over a disputed boundary. In Book 13, an arrow bounces off Menelaus' shield like chickpeas off a shovel; in the next book, a boulder by Ajax sends Hector whirling "like a whipping top"; and, in Book 15, Apollo pulls down the Greeks' rampart as casually as a boy kicking over a sandcastle. In Book 16, when Zeus' son, the Trojan ally Sarpedon, dies, warriors swarm around his body like insects around a milk pail.

There's something infinitely sad about the momentary conjuring of this distant, parallel world of children's games and peaceful farms. Homer does it once more, too, though not through a simile. In Book 22, Achilles is relentlessly chasing Hector, like a race in a nightmare, around the walls of Troy: round they go again and again . . . Suddenly Homer slows time down. Uncharacteristically, he starts to describe the surroundings: Hector and Achilles run past a wild fig tree, past the springs where the river Scamander wells up, and past the

> washing-pools
> scooped out in the hollow rocks and broad and smooth
> where the wives of Troy and all their lovely daughters
> would wash their glistening robes in the old days,
> the days of peace before the sons of Achaea came.
> *Iliad* 22 183–187

Those washing pools will never be used again. All that lies ahead for the beautiful women of Troy, with their glistening robes, is the mass slaughter of their men, enslavement, humiliation, and exile.

Herodotus and the Persian Wars

From fiction to fact: when Herodotus came to write his account of the Persian Wars, perhaps it seemed obvious: here was another example of a foreign, eastern foe being routed by an alliance of Greeks. It looked a bit, if you squinted, like another Trojan War; and this time, it was real. The very opening of Herodotus' chronicle—the first example of what we now call history—echoes the beginning of the *Iliad*. The poem starts with an invocation to sing of Achilles' rage, that rage being the cause of the destruction rained down upon the Greeks. That is to say, the words answer the question, why did all this happen? Herodotus too asks why—but in his case, he transforms a fictional probing of motivation into historical research into causation. He even notes that the Persians claim that the deep causes of the Persian Wars lay in a series of tit-for-tat abductions of women between Europe and Asia—including that of Helen of Troy. But he discards that particular interpretation as, well, fiction.

So what was the reality? At the end of the sixth century, the "ancient Greeks" were a collection of disparate, quarrelsome peoples scattered through mainland Greece, the islands of the Aegean and the Mediterranean, the tip of Italy and the west coast of what's now Turkey. And, though they were united by a common tongue, common gods, and certain important, unifying pan-Hellenic events, notably the Olympic Games, they had a limited notion of themselves as a single entity called "Greece."

The story of how these peoples, and particularly Athens, brought forth the most impressive intellectual enlightenment ever seen, throwing up great architects, playwrights, philosophers, orators, politicians, and historians, and in doing so set the cultural agenda for the West until, well, pretty much now, is inextricably linked to the Persian Wars—conflicts that saw the Greeks coming together in a small and shaky alliance of between thirty and forty *poleis* to turn away the invaders, against all the odds.

From the middle of the sixth century, a powerful empire had been growing in the Near East. The Persians, starting with King Cyrus from 550 and continuing with his successors Cambyses, Darius, and Xerxes, rapidly spread their domain from their homelands in modern Iran to what is now Turkey (including the Greek cities on the coastlands, called Ionia), to the Babylonian empire in modern Iraq, to Central Asia up to the Aral Sea, to the Indus, and to Egypt. Persia was the superpower of its day; and its incredibly wealthy, extremely sophisticated empire lasted 200 years, until Alexander the Great's sensational conquests of the 330s brought it down.

In the years between 490 and 479, Persia turned its considerable attention west to Greece. But, in a frankly fabulous turn of events, the Persians' mighty forces were held at bay and then dispatched in a series of famous battles—at Marathon, Artemisium, Thermopylae, Salamis, and Plataea. Scholars of the Near East quite rightly like to remind Hellenophiles that the Greeks were little more than an irritant to a great power that would continue to hold sway over much of the known world for generations to come. (There's a wonderful moment in Herodotus that rams this home: when the cocksure Spartans send an embassy to Cyrus to tell him to lay off the Ionian cities or else, the king of kings has to turn to a slave and inquire, "Who are the Spartans?") All this is true, but the defeat of Persia by the Greeks had extraordinary consequences for Western civilization. If mainland Greece had been drawn into the Persian empire, there would have been no rise in the power of Athens; without that dominance, the Athenian enlightenment, which produced so many of the cultural, intellectual, and artistic riches of the fifth century, almost certainly wouldn't have happened. As John Stuart Mill put it: "The battle of Marathon, even as an event in English history, is more important than the battle of Hastings."

And the history of the Persian Wars is inseparable from Herodotus, who was born in the then Greek city of Halicarnassus, now the Turkish resort of Bodrum, in about 485. The word he used to describe what he was doing, *historie*, in Greek, means "inquiry": the word history used as we understand it, as a technical term to describe an intellectual discipline or literary genre, didn't exist until Aristotle coined it later. Nonetheless, Herodotus is the true father of history (as Cicero described him) and author of what's still one of the most wonderfully entertaining, enlightening, exciting books you could have the good fortune to pick up.

Herodotus' *Histories* are a joy. His later fellow-writer, Thucydides, was miles more analytical and austere and pure in the way he wrote about events, and has undoubtedly been a more important influence on Western politicians and military strategists, but in many ways, Herodotus is richer. Herodotus' *Histories*, though they have at their heart an account of the rise of the Persian empire and the Greek resistance to its dominance, are much more than a simple historical narrative. As well as being the father of history, he can also be considered the father of ethnography, of travel writing, even of journalism. (Though we should respectfully remember that Herodotus did have his predecessors, notably the Ionian geographer and mythographer Hecataeus of Miletus, whose works are lost.)

It's only the second half of Herodotus' *Histories* that looks directly at the events of the Persian Wars. The work is organized into nine books, and from Book 5 onwards Herodotus relates the immediate circumstances leading up to the conflict, notably the "Ionian revolt," which saw the Greek cities on the Turkish west coast, which had already become part of the Persian empire, attempting to regain independence. Then, from Book 7, we have the exciting account of Xerxes' unsuccessful expedition to Greece.

The first half of the *Histories* is much more wide-ranging. At the very outset, Herodotus tells us that he wants "to preserve the fame of the important and remarkable achievements produced by both Greeks and non-Greeks" and, in particular, the "cause of hostilities between Greeks and non-Greeks." In order to do this, he begins by offering a discursive account of Persian expansionism, which is the deep, long-term cause of the Persian Wars. He kicks off by talking about the Lydian kings, including the legendarily wealthy Croesus, whose kingdom encompassed a chunk of what's now Turkey, from the Black Sea coast, south of the Sea of Marmara, down to the Greek cities on the Mediterranean. Croesus' attempted invasion of Persia ended in disaster, and in the annexation of Lydia by Cyrus. Cyrus also took on Babylon and Assyria and won; coming a cropper, eventually, when trying to conquer the savage tribe of the Massagetae. (Their queen, Tomyris, found his corpse on the battlefield, got a wineskin, filled it full of blood, and shoved his head inside it. He'd earlier tricked and killed her son by getting him drunk, so it was appropriate revenge.) The subsequent books deal with his son Cambyses' expedition against Egypt (and his eventual descent into madness); the power struggle and coup that led to Darius' becoming king; and Darius' incursions into Samos, Scythia, and Libya, before turning in earnest to the Greek world and the Ionian revolt.

What makes Herodotus such a shamelessly good read is that around and about this main thread are so many thoroughly good yarns, gossipy snippets, and psychological insights. And—this is the ethnographical side—whenever the Persians encounter a new race in order to conquer them, Herodotus will tend to pause the main narrative and give us an outline of the foreigners' history and habits, sometimes at enormous length, such that, for example, nearly the whole of Book 2 is a wonderfully arresting account of the manners and morals of the Egyptians. This is all brilliant stuff, whether he is telling us about the gold-hunting giant ants of Arabia, which are bigger than foxes but smaller than dogs; or the embalming techniques of the Egyptians (you know, scraping out the corpse's brain through the nose); or the backwards-walking cows of Libya. We'll come back to all this delicious material in chapter 6.

This business of endless digressions and pauses can make Herodotus a rather labyrinthine read, but once you get the hang of it, it works: one writer has compared the structure of his book to a washing line—there's a main thread, with fairly substantial, self-contained items hanging off it. This discursiveness has often made him the object of scorn for serious thinkers: why couldn't he just stick to the point? But arguably, the idea of this complex interconnectedness of things, people, places, and historical events is actually very sophisticated, and perhaps, in the end, more germane to the way the world works than the approaches of those historians who have seen the world simply in terms of realpolitik. And, while people's motivations in Herodotus are not always rational (his characters are as likely to be impelled by a dream, a portent, or a conversation with their wife as by calmly considered logic), often they do have the ring of psychological plausibility about them.

It is true that Herodotus' account of the world contains much that one must arch an eyebrow at. There's the scent of folktale and fable about many of his stories: in telling us about Cyrus of Persia, for instance, he starts with an account of how he was nearly killed as a baby, for his grandfather, the Mede Astyages, had dreamed that his daughter would urinate so much she would flood the whole of Asia. Worried about the metaphorical import of this (it suggested her offspring would become superpowerful, and she was married to a Persian, then a people subject to the Medes), Astyages decided to get the child killed. But the wife of the shepherd entrusted with the baby's disposal swapped him for her own stillborn infant and quietly brought him up; and Cyrus was later taken back into the royal family circle when his behavior as a boy became so noticeably kingly that his true identity was revealed. It's Moses, it's Romulus and Remus, it's Oedipus, and it's definitely too good to be true.

Some of Herodotus' yarns, on the other hand, may or may not have their basis in fact, but certainly have a marvelously bracing whiff of the tabloid newspaper report about them: take the priestess of Athena in Book 1 who, oops! grows a long bushy beard. Or, in Book 3, the story of how Babylon is finally captured, after a lengthy, stalemating siege by the Persians. The general Zopyrus tricks the Babylonians by pretending to defect to their side: as "proof" of his new allegiance, he cuts off his own ears and nose, claiming that it was done to him by the Persians. (Herodotus is said to have traveled around the Greek world giving lectures; you can just hear the audience's delighted intake of breath when he recounted episodes like this.) Frankly, it's all this stuff that makes Herodotus such fun. And in his defense, it's true that he is often skeptical himself about what he is telling us (don't necessarily believe the stuff about the one-eyed men and the gold-guarding griffins who live in the lands beyond Scythia, he helpfully warns). And, not infrequently, he gives us opposing versions of an event as it was told him by different sources. Sometimes his technique is quite close to modern newspaper reporting—placing rival accounts of events alongside each other without explicitly judging between them.

In the immediate run-up to the Persian Wars, perhaps the key event was a bold act of aggression by the Athenians. The ruler of the Ionian city of Miletus, Aristagoras, approached the mainland cities of Sparta and Athens for help in the city's revolt against Persian rule. The Spartan king turned him down. However, the newly minted democracy of Athens was easier to win round to Aristagoras' cause; he succeeded with 30,000 Athenians where he failed with just one Spartan, points out Herodotus, dryly. The Athenians duly put together a force to cross over into Asia. And, though the Persians were not a pushover, they did score a bit of a coup: they managed to burn Sardis, the former Lydian capital and then a part of the Persian empire. It was the equivalent of singeing the king of Spain's beard.

For Darius, according to Herodotus, this humiliation was not to be borne. Each day he had a slave say to him: "Master, remember the Athenians." In 490 he sent out an expeditionary force to Athens, which took the city of Eretria on the island of Euboea en route, and then landed at Marathon on the mainland. The Athenians marched east on Marathon, too, first sending a courier, Philippides, to run to Sparta—a full 140 miles, which he covered in two days—to enlist help. He received a rather typical Spartan response: yes, but not yet. Always punctilious as to religious rite and ritual, the Spartans said they could send a force only after the new moon, some days off. Amazingly, though, without Spartan reinforcements, the Athenians, aided by a troop from the town of Plataea, beat back the Persians. Their so-called "hoplite" soldiers, with bristling spears and near-impenetrable walls of shields, had proved surprisingly, and devastatingly, effective. Immediately after the battle had been decided, the exhausted Athenians rushed back home to secure their city, fearing an enemy detachment might have been sent on there: that twenty-six miles became what we know as the marathon, the race invented by Michel Bréal for the 1896 Olympics. Legend has it that Philippides ran back to Athens and died of exhaustion on the spot.

The humiliated Persians returned home and, in 486, Darius died, leaving the empire to his son Xerxes. Darius had been preparing for a full-scale invasion of Greece and now Xerxes, after dealing with an interruption in the form of a rebellion in Egypt, got on with the job. He wanted, according to Herodotus, to capture Athens and "put it to the torch."

Xerxes led his armies over the Hellespont on a vast pontoon bridge—a feat of engineering completed only on the second attempt, the first bridge having been destroyed in a storm. After that first disaster, Xerxes ordered the sea to be given 300 lashes, and hurled a pair of shackles into the water—an act of foolishness that's a key example, for Herodotus, of Xerxes overstepping the mark, displaying the kind of violent pride, or hubris, that could lead only to his downfall.

Meanwhile, more and more Greek-speaking nations defected to the Persians as the army advanced, giving in to the ritual demand for earth and water that signaled submission to the great king. (According to Herodotus, though, Xerxes didn't bother sending diplomats to Athens or Sparta: when his father had done so they had been summarily murdered.) Some Greek nations, though, including the Athenians, realized that the only way to save themselves was through unity, and they banded together under the natural authority of the best soldiers, the warlike Spartans. For the first time, there was a notion of united Greeks fighting for a common purpose: freedom.

Still, the Athenians were in a state of confusion. The Delphic oracle had advised them to trust in their "wall of wood." But that—like many utterances of the oracle—was open to interpretation. Perhaps it meant they should build a defensive blockade on the Acropolis? Or was it time to put their newly built navy to the test? A canny politician named Themistocles convinced them that the oracle meant the latter. This was the man who had recently persuaded his fellow citizens to build 200 ships, using the proceeds of the city's successful silver-mining operations.

Meanwhile, the Greeks decided to defend Thermopylae—a narrow pass, which at some points could only accommodate a single chariot—between the mountains and the Gulf of Malis. This was to be the scene of one of the most glorious military defeats in history: the battle that saw 300 Spartans under King Leonidas, together with around 6,000 allies, hold off the full might of Xerxes' infantry until an act of treachery saw them brought down and slaughtered almost to a man.

The Persian infantry advanced to Thermopylae. Xerxes is said to have sent a scout to spy on the Spartans, who saw them exercising naked and combing their long locks. Xerxes laughed at this display of apparent effeminacy: but he was about to get a dreadful shock. Battle raged at Thermopylae for two days—but there was no breakthrough. The Persian numerical superiority was useless in the confined space of the pass and against the grim professionalism and determination of the Spartans. "It was quite clear they were the experts, and that they were fighting against amateurs," said Herodotus. Xerxes withdrew his Medes and deployed the Persian elite troops called the Immortals (so called because every time one was killed he would be immediately replaced).

Still no breakthrough. But . . . there was that weak spot: the mountain path, known only to a few herdsmen, that wound up through the precipitous heights and down again behind the Spartans' position. Devastatingly, the Greeks were betrayed. One Ephialtes, a local man from Malis hoping for a rich reward from Xerxes, guided the Persians along it. When it became clear that the Greeks were surrounded, and thus absolutely doomed, Leonidas let the allies go. Now it was just the Spartans—alone. Eat a good breakfast, Leonidas is supposed to have said to his men, for tonight we dine in the Underworld.

HOPLITES AND TRIREMES

The Greeks' astounding military success against the Persians may in part be attributed to the development of a highly effective system of heavily armed infantry fighting by so-called "hoplites." The word hoplite probably took its name from the word *hopla*, which means arms and armour. The armor consisted of a round wooden shield, metal helmet, greaves, breastplate, and a spear plus sword. The effectiveness of the hoplite depended on his deployment in a phalanx—a formation, eight or sixteen men deep, in which the right side of each soldier would be protected by his neighbor's shield. In tight formation the soldiers would present a closed "box" of shields and a bristling frill of spears. In Athens, possession of a certain amount of property and the ability to afford a full set of armor meant service as a hoplite in the citizen army (the rise of hoplite fighting has also been linked to enhanced constitutional rights for non-aristocrats). In Sparta, hoplite fighting reached its apogee; its ferociously drilled, professional army was the most formidable in Greece. Hoplite fighting was a system that relied on never breaking ranks, on complete loyalty, and on utter discipline—ideals the Spartan state put at its very heart.

Another key factor in the Greeks' victory against the Persians was Athens' navy that, with ships from other Greek allies, saw off the enemy at Salamis. Athens built 200 state-of-the-art ships in the 480s with the proceeds of its state-owned silver-mining interests. These ships were triremes: highly maneuverable vessels with three banks of oars positioned one above the other, and a bronze battering ram on the prow. Later in the century, Athens' navy was to safeguard her considerable maritime empire. The triremes' rowers were mainly lower-class Athenians, as well as slaves. The rise in importance of the navy has been linked to the increased radicalization of the Athenian constitution, as the poorer members of the citizen body gained more leverage to influence political affairs.

After the three days of battle, only two of the 300 survived. Aristodamus, who had been sick during the fighting, made his way home to Sparta, where he was met with appalled disdain. His dishonor was made up for only by his heroism in the battle of Plataea. The other, Pantites, had been couriering a message to Thessaly during the battle. He hanged himself in shame. The memorial to the battle, in Herodotus' time, read:

Stranger, go and tell the people of Sparta
That we who lie here obeyed their orders.

The Persians marched into central Greece, their navy taking a parallel path over water. The war turned to the sea. The Greeks managed to hold off a storm-battered Persian fleet at Artemisium, but the battle was indecisive. Where to engage the Persians? The Peloponnesian Greeks were desperate to protect their cities, but Themistocles persuaded the Spartan admiral, Eurybiades, that the Greek naval forces should aim to fight off the island of Salamis, to which the people of Athens had been evacuated; that it would be suicide to allow the fleet to break up, each contingent rushing off to protect its own homelands. Meanwhile, Xerxes was raging through Attica and burned Athens to the ground. At the same time, the Peloponnesians were trying to build a defensive wall across the Isthmus (Greece's narrow "waist," separating the Peloponnese from the rest of the mainland) to protect the land routes. Despite Themistocles' persuasive arguments, the Peloponnesian navies still showed signs of wanting to slip away—why should they fight for Athenian territory?—so in a typically duplicitous move, he forced their hand by sending a slave of his, pretending to be sympathetic to the Persian cause, to get Xerxes' navy to strike. It worked: now there was no choice. Battle was begun.

For Xerxes, it was a fiasco. Engaging the Greeks in the straits between Salamis and the mainland was a tactical error, the confined space greatly advantageous to the allied forces. He had also been tricked by what looked like a squadron of Greek ships in flight: in fact, it was the Corinthian fleet that had sailed out of sight on a reconnaissance mission, only to turn around and attack once the king's fleet had been tempted, in its overconfidence, to enter the straits. Some of his force fought with distinction (or at least pragmatism—not least Queen Artemisia of Halicarnassus—see chapter 4). But Xerxes' crack squadrons from Phoenicia, famous for its seamanship, were rendered useless: they were crowded together and forced back to the shore by the Athenians.

And still, despite that ringing victory, it wasn't finished. Xerxes crossed back over the Hellespont with the fleet, but he left a huge army under the general Mardonius to linger into the following campaigning season of 479. An uneasy stalemate ensued, broken only when Mardonius sent King Alexander of Macedon to the ruins of Athens to set out the Persians' terms: if the Athenians gave way to Xerxes, they would be guaranteed his great favor. The Athenians refused, and, for the second time in a year, packed up and left what now passed for their city. Mardonius and his troops duly torched it—again. The Athenians sent desperate embassies to Sparta to seek help: the Spartans were on the march north to join with Athens and the other allies. The two armies met near Plataea in Boeotia, where the brilliant, disciplined, implacable hoplite army of Sparta ensured victory—and the death of Mardonius. It was over. And it was nothing less than a miracle.

300: FANTASY, FICTION, FACT

Zak Snyder's entertaining 2007 film *300*, about the battle of Thermopylae, was a highly imaginative construction. No, Xerxes was not shaven-headed, with multiple body-piercings; nor did the Greeks have to fight magical rhinoceroses. Nor, alas, did Spartans actually wear tight leather knickers. The traitor Ephialtes, who showed the Persians the mountain pass round the back of the Greek defensive position, was not a crazed Spartan outcast, but a man from Malis, near Thermopylae, hungry for Persian gold. However for all its stylization, *300* got plenty right. Yes, the Spartans ran the only professional army in Greece, head and shoulders above any other state's. Yes, the soldiers wore red cloaks and had long hair. Yes, they brought up their children solely to become good fighters, separating boys from their parents at seven and putting them through ultra-tough training and initiation rituals, even depriving them of food so they had to steal. Yes, the Spartans were famous for their educated, articulate women. The film failed, however, to mention the tradition, indeed institution, of homosexual love between the ranks. Nor did we have any shots of the Spartans' famous naked exercise routines. Gratifyingly, however, many of the best lines in *300* were actually attributed to the Spartans in antiquity, including Gorgo's "Come back with your shield, or on it"; and the warning about Persia's rains of arrows blotting out the sun being countered by the Spartan *bon mot*: "Good, for we shall be able to fight in the shade."

Thucydides and the Peloponnesian War

Greece was free. What next? The most important consequence of the Persian Wars was the extraordinary rise to prominence of Athens. The dominance of that city within Greece, and the building up of its empire (albeit a paltry thing compared with the vast Persian realms) was to have profound implications for Greece, and for later history.

After the end of the Persian Wars, the Greek allies kept up a joint army, for fear of an ongoing Persian threat. It was under the command of the Spartan king Pausanias, but, having offended the Ionian cities in the league, he was stripped of his command, and the upstart Athenians took over. This alliance became known as the Delian League, since its treasury was on the island of Delos.

However, things turned nasty. The league became completely dominated by Athens, which drew in tribute from each state, and controlled the monies. In 454 the treasury was moved to Athens itself. Bad things happened to those who decided not to cooperate: for instance, when the island of Naxos tried to secede from the league it was violently crushed by Athens. Such tensions eventually led to the Peloponnesian War, whose true cause, according to Thucydides, was "the growth of Athenian power and the fear this caused in Sparta."

The first phase of the war started in 431. It was provoked by a row between the city of Corcyra on Corfu and its colony Epidamnus. (The "age of colonization," between the eighth and the sixth centuries, had seen numerous *poleis* in Greece send groups of citizens to establish cities in other parts of the Mediterranean, settlements that tended to retain ties to their mother city.) Corcyra was itself a colony of Corinth, and Epidamnus now sought help against Corcyra from its "grandmother" city, Corinth. Athens was unwilling to allow Corinth to crush Corcyra and acquire another fleet, and so she was sucked into the conflict. This first phase of the war rumbled on for a decade, and ended more or less in a draw. Athens had scored some sensational successes, notably in Pylos, where 120 Spartan soldiers were actually captured and taken prisoner—to the shock of everyone, perhaps not least the Athenians. For once, the Spartan ideal of "never surrender" had not been achieved. In 422–1, a barely honored peace was established, bringing to an end what is called the Archidamian War (after King Archidamus of Sparta).

But hostilities broke out again in 414, when Athens embarked on a direct attack against Spartan territory by sea. They also undertook a disastrous expedition against Sicily—a preemptive strike to try to limit the island's growing power—narrated in Books 6 and 7 of Thucydides' account. The sea battle of Syracuse ended in a crushing defeat for Athens. Back home, the resultant political turbulence led to democracy being briefly abandoned, with a coup bringing in the so-called "regime of the 400," in 411. Thucydides' narrative breaks off in mid-sentence during his account of that year, but the war rumbled on until 404, when, after a siege that saw Athenians dying of starvation in the streets, Sparta finally dismantled Athens' walls and neutered her navy. Democracy—the political system that had, after all, gotten them into this mess—was again overthrown and a brutal regime known as the Thirty Tyrants took over. For some, that moment marks the passing of Athens' finest hour; nonetheless, democracy was restored in 403, and Athens after the war was still the Athens of shining-bright intellectual achievement, the Athens of Plato.

As Herodotus is to the Persian Wars, so Thucydides is to the Peloponnesian. (In fact, if some historians are greater than their material, then Thucydides is, arguably, one of them.) But the two writers couldn't be more different. Thucydides, who was born in about 460, is as austere and analytical as Herodotus is gossipy. Thucydides—not for nothing was he a favourite of Machiavelli—described the world in terms of competition for power, the rise of the strong, the failure of the weak. He himself was a general who fought for Athens during the first phase of the war; he recorded military encounters with a coolly professional eye, and an apparent unblinking objectivity (including his own unsuccessful attempt to secure the town of Amphipolis, in Thrace, after which he was exiled from Athens). His reportage skills can be thrilling. His account of the grotesque plague that harried Athens in 430, for example, is minutely and vividly observed: "The bodies of the dying were heaped one on top of the other, and half-dead creatures could be seen staggering about in the streets or flocking around the fountains in their desire for water. The temples in which they took up their quarters were full of the dead bodies of people who had died inside them . . ." Thucydides gave a very thorough description of this affliction—which he himself caught—so, he said, that it might be recognized in the future. It is a historical irony that no one has ever quite agreed on what this disease might in fact have been. The battles, too, are told with wonderful panache: the awful defeat of Athens at Syracuse is a tour de force. Here is a sample:

All the time that one ship was bearing down upon another, javelins, arrows, and stones were shot or hurled on to it without cessation by the men on the decks; and once the ships met, the soldiers fought hand to hand, each trying to board the enemy. Because of the narrowness of the space, it often happened that a ship was ramming and being rammed at the same time, and that two, or sometimes more, found themselves jammed against one, so that the steersmen had to think of defence on one side and attack of the other and, instead of being able to give their attention to one point at a time, had to deal with many different things in all directions; and the great din of all these ships crashing together was not only frightening in itself, but also made wreckage.

History of the Peloponnesian War 7 70
Translation: Rex Warner

The aftermath of this battle is horribly poignant: the Athenians retreat leaving not only the dead unburied, but abandoning the wounded and sick to their fate, who cry out and beg not to be left behind . . . "No Hellenic army had ever suffered such a reverse. They had come to enslave others, and were going away frightened of being enslaved themselves," wrote Thucydides.

Thucydides is scornful of the methods of his predecessor, Herodotus—who was "less interested in telling the truth than in catching the attention." He writes (with some justice): "It may well be that my history will seem less easy to read because of the absence in it of a romantic element." By "romantic element," he means Herodotus' myth-tinged storytelling about the distant past. My account, on the other hand, will be the truth, says Thucydides, and will provide a guide to future human action. It is not a piece of entertainment, but something that is designed to last forever. Unlike Herodotus, he does not reveal his sources, but delivers his accounts with lofty finality: he himself has ascertained the accuracy of his versions of events, either by being present himself, or consulting eyewitnesses, he claims.

One of the most striking aspects of his technique is his way of putting speeches into his characters' mouths: not what they did say, he points out, but what they might, or indeed ought, to have said. This admittedly peculiar technique gives rise to some of the most gripping writing in Greek, such as Pericles' famous funeral oration of

431, in which the statesman pays tribute to his city's dead and brilliantly lays out the fundamentals of Athenian state ideology, stirring and sinister by turns to the modern reader. Also in speech mode, Thucydides gives us the famous "Melian Dialogue," in which a delegation from Athens confronts the council of the hitherto neutral island of Melos about its refusal to come to heel as part of the empire. The Athenians argue for Melian capitulation on the unpleasant basis that they are the stronger party—so the islanders have no choice. The Melians disagree, and this thoroughly unedifying episode ends with an Athenian blockade of the island and a Melian surrender. The Athenians massacre all the men of the island and enslave the women and children.

Thucydides is the politician's historian, the soldier's historian. If the *Iliad* is read at West Point, then it will come as no surprise that so is Thucydides, and that the historian has often been drawn on by military strategists seeking to justify, explain, or critique contemporary conflicts. In the 1970s, Admiral Stansfield Turner introduced Thucydides to the syllabus of the US Naval War College, and invited the great American classicist Bernard Knox to lecture there. Knox talked about the relationship between human nature, war, empire, and democracy in Thucydides. The achievements and values of Athens justified her empire, and its loss was a tragedy. Bad leadership could mean that a great democracy could get embroiled in disastrous military campaigns, like Athens in Sicily—or, it would not take a genius to work out, America in Vietnam.

There is a delicious, but I am sure entirely apocryphal story, that Margaret Thatcher read him during the Falklands crisis (Goose Green as Pylos—too good to be true). She certainly quoted him from time to time: "The strong do what they will and the weak suffer what they must," she reminded the United Nations in 1985; a very Thatcherite sentiment, straight from the mouths of the Athenians as they lay down the law in Melos. Gordon Brown is a Thucydidean, too, in his way. As a child he was taken to see Edinburgh's war memorial by his father. The inscription, from Pericles' funeral oration, had a lasting impact on him, or so he recounts in his book on war heroes. "The whole earth is the tomb of heroes and their story is not graven in stone over their clay, but abides everywhere, without visible symbol, woven into the stuff of other men's lives," were the words he found so affecting. It seems less likely that George W. Bush knows his Thucydides, but an American commentator pointed out in 2004 that one of his speechwriters did, so reminiscent of Bush's utterances of the time seemed these words from Thucydides' Corinthians: "Do not delay, fellow-allies, but convinced of the necessity of the crisis, and the wisdom of our advice, vote for the war, undeterred by its immediate terrors, but looking beyond to the lasting peace by which it will be succeeded. War makes peace more secure."

The Peloponnesian War itself, as it dragged on, became controversial and sometimes deeply unpopular in Athens, a fact reflected in plays produced at the time. Aristophanes' comedy *Acharnians*, performed in 425, is about an ordinary Athenian, Dicaeopolis, who negotiates a private peace; his *Lysistrata* of 411 is about the women of Greece going on sex strike to get their men to end the conflict.

And then there were tragedies, such as *The Trojan Women* by Euripides. This play looked at the ghastly fate of the women of Troy after the sacking of their city: what you might call the "collateral damage." The play dares to confront head-on perhaps the most horrific moment of the Trojan War—when Hector and Andromache's young son Astyanax is thrown over the battlements of the city and killed—a deed that is foreshadowed in the *Iliad*. The drama examines the erosion of morality in war, what it means to be a soldier or official asked to complete orders that have no foundation in what is right. Its original production was in 415, shortly after the Melian massacre, and it is hard not to infer pointed comment on that dreadful event by Euripides. In our war-stricken era, it is a drama that seems timely depressingly often.

War was, like it or not, part and parcel of the Greek experience. Perhaps it was the fate of this uneasily disposed jigsaw of independent states, competing for resources and for power, to fight each other. And, on that extraordinary occasion when a collection of Greek states set aside their rivalries to vanquish a common enemy, they pulled off a miraculous victory that still reverberates down the millennia. Through Homer, Herodotus, and Thucydides, and through the playwrights, especially Euripides, the Greeks have handed down to us the richest books about war the world has produced—from the adventure and derring-do of Herodotus, to the tough-minded realpolitik of Thucydides, to the unblinking confrontation of wartime atrocities of Euripides. The *Iliad* stands at the head of all these books: in its vision of war's camaraderie, glory, pain, loss, pity, grief, and, at times, senselessness, it has never known an equal.

6. Beyond the borders:
Greeks and barbarians

HERE ARE THE opening lines of the *Odyssey*:

> Sing to me of the man, Muse, the man of twists and turns
> driven time and again off course, once he had plundered
>   the hallowed heights of Troy.
> Many cities of men he saw and learned their minds,
> many pains he suffered, heartsick on the open sea,
> fighting to save his life and bring his comrades home.
>
> *Odyssey* 1 1–6

"Many cities of men he saw and learned their minds." Poor old Odysseus: all he wanted to do was to get back home to his Penelope again, instead of which he was blown off course to all kinds of unknown and dangerous locations, involving randy goddesses, hungry, multiheaded monsters and, in the case of the cattle of the sun-god Helios, tempting walking dinners that his hapless crew on no account should have tucked into . . . And he did, as he went, see a great deal: the *Odyssey* is perfumed with salty travelers' tales, sailors' yarns, tall tales from beyond the horizon.

111

Mainland Greece has a magnificently jagged coastline, and the Aegean is polka-dotted with innumerable islands: the Greeks were, unsurprisingly, seafaring people. And they were colonizers, too: from around the eighth century, Greek settlements were established right across the Mediterranean from the south of France and southern Italy to Ionia, on the west coast of what's now Turkey. Homer himself was said by some in antiquity to come from the Ionian island of Chios.

The Greek word "barbarian," which means foreigner, probably derives (paradoxically) from a Babylonian word, *barbaru*: it refers to "incomprehensible speech" and is onomatapoeic—those foreigners, all they say is "bar-bar-bar-bar." Philologists have linked it to the word baby, another species of human whose burblings we cannot understand. The point is that non-Greekness of non-Greeks relates to their language, not to their location. The Greeks got around: they were so widely scattered that a term like "overseas" wouldn't be any use if you wanted to describe foreigners.

Homer refers to some of the Trojan allies as *barbarophonoi*, "bar-bar-speaking," but it was after foreigners had shaped themselves into something sinister—the Enemy, in the guise of the big bad Persian menace—that the word "barbarian" began to mean something rather particular. The defeat of the Persians arguably gave the Greeks something like self-consciousness as a single people, a people who could, on occasion, unite against a common foe—even if the notion had a tinge of wishful thinking about it, given that the shaky Greek alliance that triumphed in the Persian Wars consisted of around forty Greek states out of more than 1,000. It is in Aeschylus' history play, *The Persians*, produced in 472, that we see the germ of the "barbarian" of popular Greek caricature: a freedom-hating, slavish, decadent, luxurious, cruel coward. It is a stereotype that has left a long shadow, for this is arguably the root of orientalism, the notion of the East as an exotic realm that harbors dangerous pleasures and fosters despotism; the "supine" East, as John Buchan put it.

Apart from their funny way of speaking, the other point of the barbarians is that they were literally everyone else except the Greeks: any old foreigners lumped into one great mass of Otherness. The Greeks loved their contrasts, their opposites. Man is the opposite of (and is superior to) woman. The free man is the opposite of (and is superior to) the slave. The Greek is the opposite of (and is superior to) the barbarian. The Greek language itself helps. Two of the most common words in ancient Greek are *men* and *de*, which are usually clunkily translated as "on the one hand" and "on the other hand." With the aid of these delightfully terse monosyllables, the Greeks cooked up contrasts and opposites by the bucketload. The barbarians are everything that the Greeks are not. Take this passage from *Airs, Waters, Places*, a treatise from the *Hippocratic Corpus* (see chapter 7), which explains how your physical location affects your health. Funnily enough, the topography of Greece tends to produce by far the best kind of people, according to this (unknown) author:

> You will find, as a general rule, that the constitutions and the habits of a people follow the nature of the land where they live. Where the soil is rich, soft and well-watered and where surface water is drunk, which is warm in summer and cold in winter, and where the seasons are favourable, you will find the people fleshy, their joints obscured, and they have watery constitutions. Such people are incapable of great effort. In addition, such a people are, for the most part, cowards. They are easy-going and sleepy, clumsy craftsmen and never keen or delicate. But if the land is bare, waterless and rough, swept by the winter gales and burnt by the summer sun, you will find there a people hard and spare, their joints showing, sinewy and hairy. They are by nature keen and fond of work, they are wakeful, headstrong and self-willed

and inclined to fierceness rather than tame. They are keener at their crafts, more intelligent and better warriors.

Airs, Waters, Places
Translation: J. Chadwick and W. N. Mann

But this is to run ahead of Homer, from whom such stereotypes are, for the most part, absent. Instead, it was the age of colonization that left its traces in the composition of the Homeric epics. In Odysseus' description of the Cyclopes' island you can feel an echo of the potential settler sizing up a good-looking site:

No mean spot,
it could bear you any crop you like in season.
The water-meadows, along the low foaming shore
run soft and moist, and your vines would never flag.
The land's clear for ploughing. Harvest on harvest,
a man could reap a healthy stand of grain—
the subsoil's dark and rich.

Odyssey 6 143–9

This part of the story is told in flashback: Odysseus is narrating his earlier adventures to the friendly, if sometimes rather intimidating Phaeacians, on the last stop before he finally makes it home.

The Phaeacians, though in some ways a tricky lot, are generous hosts who give Odysseus a ship and a crew, load him down with treasure, and get him home in the end. But (like a less glamorous Blanche DuBois) Odysseus depends on the kindness of strangers. Every unknown shore could mean an encounter with a friend . . . or a foe. He could be waylaid by a charming, attractive young princess, as he is when he washes up on the Phaeacians' beach. Or very nearly eaten for dinner, as happens chez Polyphemus, the Cyclops.

"Man of misery, whose land have I lit on now?
What are they here—violent, savage, lawless?
or friendly to strangers, god-fearing men?"

Odyssey 6 131–3

That's what Odysseus moans to himself when he reaches Phae-acia, having narrowly escaped the heaving waves and blasting winds sent by the furious Poseidon. No wonder there's a note of desperation in his voice: by this time he's experienced every possible welcome, and has been greeted by hosts good and bad . . . but mostly bad.

The guest-host relationship in Homer, and, indeed, forward through the the centuries into classical Greece, was an institution of great importance. Zeus himself protected the sacred bond between guest and host, and if a stranger turned up on your doorstep, you were to treat him well, feed him, give him a bed, and ideally send him on his way loaded with gifts (which always feels odd to modern ears, since for us it's guests, not hosts, who tend to bring a present). In a society that was pretty mobile, but lacking in what we would recognize as the basic infrastructure of travel (hotels, inns), you can see how the guest-host relationship had a very practical basis. But even more importantly, the bonds made in this ritualized form of friendship could be powerful, almost like political alliances. In Book 6 of the *Iliad*, Diomedes and Glaucus, who are on opposite sides in the Trojan War, decide not to fight each other, and instead exchange armor, because their ancestors were guest-friends.

In the *Odyssey*, that travel-heavy poem, a character's hostly quali-ties provide a sure-fire guide to his or her moral worth. When Telema-chus sails away from Ithaca in search of news of his father, at the beginning of the poem, he visits his father's old comrades-in-arms Nestor and Menelaus, in Pylos and Sparta respectively. Menelaus is a delightful host, though overzealous: he wants to keep Telemachus at

Sparta for a year, and give him a team of horses. Telemachus gently points out that he cannot stay a year and horses are no good on the rocky isle of Ithaca. Conceding graciously, Menelaus presents him instead with a mixing bowl made by the god Hephaestus and given to him by the king of Sidon (re-gifting is clearly not a social gaffe in the Homeric world). As in hosting, so in life: we are shown that Menelaus is generous to a fault, and perhaps a touch thoughtless. It's a sign of Telemachus' rising maturity that he can deal so gracefully with a potentially awkward host-guest scenario.

Odysseus, too, has to deal with a host who is just a bit too hospitable, though on quite a different scale: Calypso. The nymph just won't let him leave her island home, with the result that he is stuck there for seven years: this is where we find him at the beginning of the poem, when Athena decides it's time to give him a helping hand. Admittedly, it could be worse: Calypso's cave comes with five-star accommodation and gastronomy, and she even offers to make Odysseus immortal, which you don't get every day. But Odysseus is pining to get home to his Ithaca and his Penelope. In the end, it is only a message from Hermes, hotfooting it from Zeus, that persuades Calypso to release her houseguest (frankly, if she weren't so charming and delightful, there'd be something of the Kathy Bates in *Misery* about her).

Odysseus has a tricky time of it with another formidable demigoddess, this time on the marvelously vowelly, palindromic island of Aeaea. Landing there, he sends an advance-guard of his men to look for signs of life. When they find a house and knock on the door, the rather terrifying Circe appears and turns them, inexplicably, into pigs (not, I think, a move recommended by Miss Manners). Odysseus escapes the same fate only by dint of eating a magical herb and threatening the witch with his sword. After that, Circe turns into quite the hostess with the mostest. Odysseus and his crew enjoy it so much they stay for a year.

116

These unpredictable ladies, though, are far from the worst of it. The Laestrygonians are cannibals who dine off Odysseus' fleet in Book 10 of the poem; his own ship is the only one to escape. And then there's Polyphemus, the Cyclops. When Odysseus and his comrades get trapped inside Polyphemus' cave after yet another inland foray from an unknown shore, he calls on the creature to respect Zeus' host-guest laws, but Polyphemus just laughs in his face. His guest-gift to Odysseus, he says, will be to eat him—last.

When Odysseus finally reaches Ithaca, he is a stranger on his own home island, too: or at least, thickly disguised as an old beggar, he purports to be, until he reveals himself to the suitors who have been harrying Penelope. This disguise gives him the perfect way of testing out the moral worth of his people. He gets to discover not only how they treat strangers, left to their own devices, but also how they *really* feel about their long-absent king. His old swineherd Eumaeus scores top marks. He is desperately poor, but without knowing who this scruffy newcomer really is, treats him as much like a king as he can: welcomes him, cooks for him, and goes cold at night so his guest can have a cloak to sleep in. His behavior is in absolute contrast to that of the suitors at Odysseus' palace, who not only abuse their position as guests—eating Telemachus and Penelope out of house and home, behaving with rudeness and lack of consideration—but are also appalling hosts, treating the beggar Odysseus with utter contempt.

"Many cities of men he saw and learned their minds"—the most celebrated Greek who did this for real was, of course, the estimable Herodotus, father of history, and the original foreign correspondent. His *Histories* contain rich and fascinating descriptions of worlds and peoples beyond the borders of the Greeks, among them Egypt, Libya, Ethiopia, and Arabia; Lydia, Assyria, and Persia; Scythia and Thrace. He didn't travel to absolutely everywhere he talks about, but he did seemingly cover an astonishing amount of ground—he describes things he has seen with his own eyes on the river Dnieper in

Russia; alludes to inquiries undertaken in southern Italy, the shores of the Black Sea, and Libya; and sets down the fruit of extensive researches in Egypt.

Herodotus tells us he questioned locals he met on his travels, but he spoke only Greek, and so relied on interpreters; unsurprisingly, he filtered everything he learned through his very Greek way of looking at the world. There is, therefore, a great deal of highly entertaining nonsense in his accounts. However, there is also an enormous amount that is absolutely commonsensical and spot on—including some very well-observed comments on the geography and natural history of the Nile, and accounts of the habits of the Scythians that, far-fetched as they can appear, seem to have been borne out by modern archaeology. He also tries to be evenhanded and dispassionate, though it's clear he has his favorite peoples and places (the Egyptians score pretty highly: he obviously admires their ancient, complex, and clever civilization). Perhaps the most outlandish and hilarious story—just beating out the lovely anecdote about the Arabian sheep whose tails are so long they have little carts to drag them around on—is about the giant ants who harvest gold. These marvelous creatures from India are "bigger than foxes, although they never reach the size of dogs." They burrow underground to make their nests and bring the precious metal up to the surface. It sounds bonkers, but, to be sure, a serious article in *New Scientist* magazine in 2007 remarked how termites, which burrow up to thirty meters deep into the earth, leave traces of precious minerals in their mounds in precisely the same way as that described by Herodotus. Furthermore, said the article, geologists in Australia now regard the insects as "the ticket to new reserves of diamonds, gold, and other buried treasure." Subsequent correspondence in the magazine pointed out Herodotus' prescience. All right, termites may not be quite the size of foxes—perhaps there was some muddle with his interpreters.

And Herodotus, crucially, is rather too sophisticated a thinker to fall quite neatly into the Greeks = brilliant, barbarians = villains formula. His foreigners do bear traces of the caricatured qualities I mentioned above—but there are plenty of wise, sensible barbarians in his *Histories*; and, notwithstanding his Hellenocentrism, a strikingly relativist view of the manners and mores of the barbarians. "If one were to order all mankind to choose the best set of rules in the world, each group would, after due consideration, choose its own customs; each group regards its own as being the best by far," he writes. He sets out a (truly bizarre) anecdote from the Persian court as evidence for this radical thought:

> During Darius' reign, he invited some Greeks who were present to a conference, and asked them how much money it would take for them to be prepared to eat the corpse of their fathers; they replied that they would not do it for any amount of money. Next, Darius summoned some members of the Indian tribe known as Callatiae, who eat their parents, and asked them in the presence of the Greeks . . . how much money it would take for them to be willing to cremate their fathers' corpses; they cried out in horror and told him not to say such appalling things.
>
> *Histories* 3 38
> Translation: Robin Waterfield

He concludes by quoting the poet Pindar: "custom is king." Travel, one suspects, had indeed broadened the mind in Herodotus' case.

Sometimes, he even sounds a little like a tour guide (just the sort you want, who gives you the juicy details about what the king and queen said to each other in bed the night of the revolution, as well as telling you the dimensions of the local architectural masterpieces). If Herodotus had been running Swan Hellenic cruises, perhaps they would have looked something like this . . .

Egypt and the Nile

We view the pyramids, Egypt's most noteworthy monuments. (Note: because of the idiosyncratic climate and geography of this country, nearly all Egyptian customs are the opposite of those anywhere else. For instance, women go out and sell goods in the market; men stay at home and do the weaving. Women urinate standing up; men do so squatting.) Nature lovers will enjoy the sight of crocodiles and hippopotami along the Nile, and, for the bird watchers among us, there is a chance to see a phoenix—though, alas, they appear only at 500-year intervals. Perhaps instead we shall catch a glimpse of the flying snakes of Arabia, if any have by chance managed to avoid the predatory ibises as they make their way toward Egypt.

Suggested extras: a trip to an embalmer's premises: watch the locals prepare their dead for the afterlife.

Ethiopia

A visit to the Table of the Sun, a field in which meat of every conceivable animal is spontaneously produced by the earth overnight. Apparently.

The Black Sea

An adventurous encounter with the strikingly lawless, nomadic Scythians. On our first night we enjoy a typically meaty local meal. The unique, completely waste-free Scythian "self-cooking" cuisine sees an animal's flesh boiled in a vessel fashioned from the creature's own skin and cooked on a fire made from its own bones. An opportunity to admire the Scythians' distinctive local dress: coats made from human scalps.

Shopping: unusual souvenirs include quiver-covers made from the skin of human arms.

Optional visit to a Scythian religious ceremony. (Warning: human sacrifice may be involved; the company takes no responsibility for the security of individuals aboard the MS *Halicarnassus*, etc. etc. . . .)

Well, I think it sounds like a lovely holiday.

Herodotus—and specifically the Herodotus of the exotic and the foreign, rather than the Herodotus of the Persian Wars—enjoyed a considerable surge in popularity after the late Anthony Minghella's 1996 film of Michael Ondaatje's novel *The English Patient*. If you'll remember, Almásy always carries with him his copy of Herodotus. A surveyor, explorer, and mapper of the Sahara, Almásy (the smoldering Ralph Fiennes) would "often open Herodotus for a clue to geography." A newly married couple, Katharine and Geoffrey Camps, join Almásy on an expedition. Around the fire one night, Katharine, played by the gorgeous Kristin Scott Thomas, tells the story of Candaules' wife—a story that occurs in the first book of Herodotus' *Histories*.

The story goes like this. Candaules, King of Lydia, fell in love with his own wife. He told his favorite, Gyges, all about her beauty, but in the end he said, "Gyges, I don't think you really believe me. I'm going to find a way for you to see her naked." Gyges protested at the perverseness of this idea. But Candaules insisted, saying that he would contrive the whole business so that the queen wouldn't know what was going on. "Just hide behind the open door of the bedroom. I'll be there already, and she will have her back to you as she undresses. Then you can slip out of the door." With deep misgivings, Gyges did as he was told. Candaules' wife did indeed spot him as he crept out of the door—but, instead of crying out, she kept quiet and pretended she hadn't seen a thing. For revenge, as they say, is a dish best served cold.

The next morning, she summoned Gyges, and told him, "Either you can kill Candaules and take both his kingdom and his wife, or you can die now, so that you can never again do to me what you did last night. This is the choice: either the man who thought of doing this is going to die, or the man who saw me naked when he should not have done." Gyges begged her not to make him make such a

121

decision, but she insisted: and he chose to live. And that is how Gyges became king of Lydia.

When Katharine tells this story in *The English Patient*, it's a fantastically charged moment: she and Almásy are going to fall deeply in love with each other, an event this story from Herodotus prefigures, or even reveals. Within the texture of the novel, the episode also reminds us how the personal and the political intertwine, how human affairs shape history.

So you can see that it's not a bad idea to have a Herodotus story, a story from beyond the borders, up your sleeve for those cold desert nights around the campfire. But which to choose? There are so many contenders. The one about the tyrant Polycrates, who threw his favorite ring into the sea only to have it served to him for dinner in a magnificent fish the next day? Or the story of Arion, the great singer, who survived a pirate-ordered plank-walking by riding a dolphin to safety? The tale of how Darius got his horse to neigh on cue, and thus won himself the throne of Persia? How Cyrus was exposed at birth but then came miraculously to light and ended up founding a great empire? Personally, I always enjoy what happened when the wise Solon—the grandfather of Athenian democracy—visited King Croesus of Lydia, Gyges' distant descendant.

Here goes. Croesus, king of Lydia, was a fantastically rich man, and a generous host. When Solon came to visit him, he arranged for the Athenian to be shown his many incredible treasures and priceless artifacts. After this dazzling tour had come to an end, Croesus said to his guest: "My dear Solon, we've heard so much about your good sense and wisdom. Tell me, have you ever come across any one man who is happier, more fortunate than everybody else?" Croesus smiled graciously at the Athenian, and cast a satisfied glance over his giant heaps of gold coins and his fabulous art collection: he confidently expected that Solon would say that *he* was the most fortunate man in the world. However, Solon replied, "Absolutely, Your Majesty. There is such a man: it is Tellus of Athens."

Croesus was rather put out: surely he, king of Lydia, was better off than some Greek who no one had ever heard of. Solon expanded, "You see, Your Majesty, it's quite simple: Tellus was a good man, pretty well off by our humble standards, who had fine sons whom he lived to see grow up. And, when Athens was at war with her neighbors, he singlehandedly saw off the enemy. He died gloriously in battle, and then he was given a wonderful funeral by the Athenians."

"Oh, I see," said Croesus, although he didn't really, and was ever so slightly put out. He said, "I wonder then, Solon, who you believe to be the second-happiest person in the world? I suppose you can't think of anyone in *particular* can you?" Solon's reply was immediate: "Absolutely no doubt about it: the second-happiest people in the world are Cleobis and Biton."

"Who?" snapped Croesus. "Not more Greeks, I trust?"

"Yes, indeed," said Solon. "The brothers Cleobis and Biton were both famous, prizewinning athletes from Argos. But that's not the reason I mention them. Once, their mother urgently needed to be taken to the sanctuary of Hera, but there were no oxen available to draw her cart. So Cleobis and Biton hitched themselves up to it, and transported her forty-five stades, an incredible achievement. Their arrival caused a sensation. The mother went right up to the statue of the goddess and prayed that her sons be rewarded with whatever it was that it was best for a human being to have. Later, the men lay down for a rest in the sanctuary—and they never got up again. They died where they lay, and the Argives had statues made of them and dedicated them at Delphi."

"Good god!" said Croesus. "You mean you really value the happiness of these ordinary citizens higher than that of a king? I'm afraid I think your wisdom has been rather overrated."

"Let me explain," said Solon. "I can see that your wealth is tremendous, your taste in art impeccable, and your realm enormous. But there are many days in a man's life—26,250, by my calculations, assuming he lives to see seventy. Not every one of those days is going to bring good luck with it. Frankly, I think you are a fortunate man, Croesus. But anything could happen to you. You could lose your throne tomorrow. To my mind, no man can be called truly happy until he has died well."

Croesus was extremely irritated by what Solon had to say, and really did decide that the Athenian's reputation for wisdom was unfounded. However, he would have been well advised to have listened to Solon. For before Croesus died, he lost his kingdom to the Persians. Perhaps it was divine punishment for imagining himself to be the happiest man on earth, who knows? And in losing his kingdom, he gave the Persians an empire, and it was as a result of the Persians' increasing power over the known world that they finally came to invade Greece . . .

7. The twilight of the gods:
The beginnings of science, from Thales to Aristotle

AT THE BEGINNING of the sixth century there lived in Miletus, in Ionia, a man called Thales. According to Plato, in his dialogue *Theaetetus*, Thales died by falling into a well while he was gazing on the heavens, poor fellow. If early Greek science can, occasionally, come under fire for being insufficiently empirical and too focused on the assertion and counterassertion of cosmological theories, then at least tradition has it that the man credited with the founding of Greek science—and philosophy—was interested, to a fault, in observing natural phenomena. You might say that Thales, not looking where he was going, also gives us the foundation myth of the mad professor, of the thinker so wrapped up in important abstractions that everyday concerns fall by the wayside.

In ancient Greece there was no word for what we would term science, as such, and the earliest thinkers, who now tend to be referred to under the umbrella term of "pre-Socratic philosophers," would likely have described what they were doing as conducting "inquiries"—which is what Herodotus the historian was doing, albeit from a slightly different perspective. What Thales and Co. had in common with Herodotus was that they tried to explore natural (or, in Herodotus' case, historical) phenomena *without* explaining them in terms of the gods or the supernatural. To begin to try to explain the world as a sequence of rationally explicable events—to say that storms at sea are not sent by Poseidon, nor lightning by Zeus— was an intellectual shift of extraordinary power, as significant as, if not more significant than, the intellectual shifts that ushered in the Reformation, or the Enlightenment. It was a move that cleared the pathways for the riches of philosophical, literary, and political developments of the fifth century and put man, rather than the gods, at the center of the universe.

Still, fans of ancient Egypt and Babylon might point out, with justice, that way before the Greeks got going, enormous advances had been made in mathematics and astronomy (a debt that Plato himself acknowledged). The Babylonians, for instance, actually had a reasonably accurate calendar, which is more than the Greeks could manage. In a typically chaotic manner, each of the Greek *poleis* had their own version of the calendar, with different names for the months, and based on a lunar system—which, of course, does not dovetail with the solar system. If you calculate your calendar on the basis of lunar months, there will be ten or so days left over each year. So every few years, if things felt out of synch, if a midsummer month didn't feel sufficiently midsummery, a city-state would simply have the month again, to even things out.

The work of the early scientists is often preserved in tiny fragments, or expressed in rather obscure and gnomic terms, or known only as quoted or summarized by later writers; piecing their theories together is a delicate, and often contentious, task. Thales put forward the theory that the world was held up by water; and that earthquakes, far from being the work of Poseidon, were the result of wave tremors from below the earth. Anaximander, another Milesian, perhaps Thales' pupil, wrote a prose treatise called *On the Nature of Things*: he is thus responsible for one of the first-preserved prose sentences in Greek. (The very first writer of Greek prose is reputed to be Pherecydes of Syros in the Cyclades, who wrote about the gods and the creation of the cosmos in the mid-sixth century.) For Anaximander, the governing principle of the world, what "held it up," was the Boundless, or the Infinite (which is an attempt to answer the question left hanging by Thales, that is, what holds the water up?). Anaximander was responsible for the first attempt in Greek astronomy to posit a mechanical model for the heavenly bodies: the earth is a flat-topped cylinder, he held, while the sun, moon, and stars are formed by hidden wheels of fire. (In other words, he proposed that what we see as a star "is like a puncture in a vast celestial bicycle wheel," as one eminent writer on Greek science puts it.) Symmetry is key to Anaximander's conception: opposites are separated out to generate the hot and the cold, the dry and the wet. His pupil, Anaximenes, who was working during the third quarter of the sixth century, proposed on the other hand that air was the primary material: as breath governs humans, so air governs the world. To explain change and world formation, he offered the idea of condensation and rarefaction of the air: air becomes fire by rarefaction, condenses to become water, and again to become stones.

Pythagoras, another Ionian—from the island of Samos, who then emigrated to Croton in Italy—is perhaps now the most celebrated of these early thinkers by reason of his famous theorem. He was at the center of a group held together by mystical religious beliefs, and he propounded the idea of the transmigration of souls, that is, the idea that a soul finds another host when a body dies. The Pythagoreans were also vegetarians (the corollary of the transmigration belief), though I worry slightly about their protein intake since they also, for reasons that are not entirely clear, eschewed legumes. (Because they make you fart? Because beans have some special role in the migration of souls? The scholarly debate rages . . .) For Pythagoras and his followers, number was the organizing principle of the universe, and they did significant work in mathematics, not surpassed until Euclid in the third century. All together now: the square on the hypotenuse of a right-angled triangle is equal to the sum of the squares on the other two sides. The Pythagoreans made important discoveries about music, too: that the intervals of an octave, a fifth, and a fourth could be expressed as simple ratios (1:2, 2:3, 3:4). But the number obsession went further than that. For the Pythagoreans, the world was, in some fundamental way, *made* from number: "the whole heaven is a musical scale and a number." From the Pythagoreans comes the idea of the "music of the spheres"—that the movements of the heavenly bodies created inaudible sounds (inaudible to all, that is, but Pythagoras himself). The universe consisted, later Pythagoreans thought, of a central fiery body around which the moons, stars, and planets revolved, plus, rather confusingly, an invisible "counter earth" that did its thing beneath our own earth. Bonkers it sounds, but it's an interesting conception in that it did, unusually, remove the earth from the center of the universe.

Also working in Italy, in Elea, south of Naples, was Parmenides. His early-fifth century poem has its narrator journey to a mysterious region where the opposites are undivided (whatever that might mean). Here he meets a goddess who reveals to him the following notion: since thought or speech must have an object, nothingness cannot figure in our thought or speech. If something is sayable or thinkable, it must *be*. So (says the goddess) not only can nothingness not figure in our speech, but neither can plurality or change, on the grounds that to talk about such things would entail using comparative and negative language . . . Zeno was an associate of Parmenides, and his famous paradoxes supported this notion of no-change. The best known is that of Achilles racing the tortoise. "In a race, the quickest runner can never overtake the slowest, since the pursuer must first reach the point whence the pursued started, so that the slower must always hold a lead." (That's Aristotle quoting the paradox.) To explain: say Achilles gives the tortoise a head start of a hundred feet. After a certain time, Achilles will reach the tortoise's starting point; but the tortoise will already have passed that point. So, whenever Achilles reaches a place that the tortoise has been, he still has further to go. Thus (contra common sense) he will never catch up with the tortoise. I will leave you with the interesting task of refuting this paradox. Knowledge of calculus might come in handy.

At the same time as Parmenides was tackling the world in terms of no-change, Heraclitus, in Ephesus, on the other side of the Mediterranean, was suggesting the opposite: that change is a dynamic force. "Everything flows," is the most famous statement attributed to him, though precisely how that might be interpreted is open to question. Fire was the basic element, he claimed, and nature was like a taut bow; even when apparently stable, it might entail tensions pulling in opposite directions.

Parmenides and Heraclitus set up, in different ways, the problem of change, which is intimately connected to what, in fact, matter *is*. (Where do things come from? In what sense do they cease to be?) Empedocles, born in about 492, proposed the four elements, earth, air, fire, and water, as the "roots" of things. Everything else was made from combinations of these basic elements in fixed proportions (and though the sort of elements he proposed were off the mark, of course, the idea that matter was formed from basic elements in fixed proportions is absolutely spot on). "Love" and "strife" were the fundamental forces that drew substances together or drove them apart. Another spirited attempt to solve the problem came from the Ionian Anaxagoras (not to be confused, of course, with our friends Anaximander and Anaximenes), who contended that everything had a bit of everything else in it: "all things have a share in all things." So, for instance, sperm contains a bit of all the flesh, blood, fingernails, bones, and so forth, of which a child consists. It must (he thought) because flesh (for example) could not spring from not-flesh.

Anaxagoras, who was born in 500-ish, moved to Athens and became Pericles' tutor. Leucippus and Democritus, working in the middle of the fifth century, had a quite different idea about how matter was formed: they propounded the idea that it was made up of tiny invisible, undividable particles. It was called the atomic theory. It didn't catch on at the time . . .

On the stargazing front, Plato was influential in insisting that astronomy should be treated as an exact, mathematical science, not reliant on observation alone. Naturally, however, observation set up the main problems. Even in the earliest works of literature, like the poetic farming manual *Works and Days*, it's clear that the movements of the stars had been observed and were used: pick your grapes, advises Hesiod, when Orion the hunter and Sirius his dog come into mid-heaven. So it had already been figured out that different constellations are visible from a given point at different seasons. It was also noted that most stars rise in the east and set in the west; and that the sun's position in relation to the stars changes regularly, progressing from west to east through a band of constellations (the zodiac) in the course of about a year. The planets, too, progress through the zodiac, but at different speeds: it takes Venus and Mercury roughly a year to take the journey, but Saturn (say) thirty years. It was also noticed that as the stars take this journey they sometimes appear to be stationary or move backwards (are retrograde), which is what astrologers are always banging on about—Mercury is retrograde in Aquarius, beware of taking planes or trains, that kind of thing. Eudoxus, working in the fourth century, did some incredibly complicated and ingenious math to try to account for this retrograde movement, setting up a model of the universe as a pattern of concentric spheres with earth at the center, and positing a figure-of-eight curve called a hippopede (literally, a horse-fetter) to explain the retrogression. (The real reason that planets are retrograde is much easier to explain if you have figured out that the sun, not the earth, is the center of the system.

Imagine a model with the sun at the center, the earth orbiting around it, and Mars also orbiting, further away from the sun. At a particular point, the earth will "overtake" Mars, a process that, viewed from the earth, would give the appearance of Mars staying put or moving backwards, for a time. Figuring all that out would have to be left to Copernicus in the sixteenth century.)

Eudoxus' theories, despite their ingenuity, have been criticized for apparently willfully flying in the face of available data. But in another branch of scientific endeavour, medicine, observation was having its day. Greek literature starts with a disease, and an attempt to heal it. In the *Iliad*, a plague, sent by Apollo, is having a devastating effect on the Greek troops. In order to propitiate the god, Agamemnon returns the daughter of a Trojan priest of Apollo, a prisoner of war. The plague abates. The Greeks also count among their number the first literary doctors: a pair of brothers, Machaon and Podalirius, the sons of Asclepius, famous for their healing skills. (The brothers appear on the Royal College of Surgeons' armorial bearings to this day, and a fine pair of fellows they are, too.) At the end of Book 11, Patroclus finds his friend Eurypylus wounded. Both Machaon and Podalirius are unavailable, Machaon wounded and in need of a doctor himself, so Patroclus rolls up his sleeves to do a bit of emergency surgery:

> Patroclus stretched him out
> knelt with a knife and cut the sharp, stabbing arrow
> out of Eurypylus' thigh and washed the wound clean
> of the dark running blood with clear warm water.
> Pounding it in his palms, he crushed a bitter root
> and covered over the gash to kill his comrade's pain,
> a cure that fought off every kind of pain . . .
> and the wound dried and the flowing blood stopped.
>
> *Iliad* 11 1008–1015

So in the *Iliad*, the practice of medicine combines notions of god-sent affliction and practical-minded field surgery. In the *Odyssey*, Helen, rather intriguingly, gives her husband Menelaus and their guests a drug that makes them forget the traumas of the Trojan War—you could see it as an early antidepressant, perhaps . . .

From about 500, a new cult began to spring up in Greek cities—that of Asclepius who, mythically, had learned his doctor's skills from Chiron the centaur. He was the god to whom you might turn to seek the alleviation of a health problem; you might sleep in his sanctuary and see what your dreams told you about a cure. But he was also a sort of patron of the medical profession—not that Greek doctors were a profession in any organized way, with recognized qualifications or anything of that sort (though the islands of Cos and Cnidus were famous for producing doctors, like Scotland in the twentieth century or Cuba now). Doctors, we can infer, probably traveled, offering care for a fee. In Herodotus, there is a Greek doctor, Democedes, who is employed by the tyrant Polycrates of Samos as the local GP for a fixed fee; he ends up treating the Persian queen Atossa for a breast tumor and then, via her, suggesting to King Darius the interesting notion of conquering the Greeks: he becomes their guide on the reconaissance mission. But the most famous of Greek doctors was, and remains, Hippocrates of Cos, regarded as the father of medicine.

Hippocrates was celebrated in his own day (the second half of the fifth century): Plato mentions him in his work *Phaedrus*. Very little is known about his life or personal achievements, but what we do have is a copious collection of medical texts dating from about 420 to 370, collectively known as the Hippocratic Corpus—some of them perhaps by Hippocrates, and most of them probably not. The names of these individual works, which range from rhetorical defenses of particular medico-scientific positions to detailed case histories to collections of surgical know-how, are a joy for their names alone: *Breaths*; *Epidemics*; *Aphorisms*; *Precepts*; *Affections*; *Airs, Waters, Places* . . . I am also rather attached to the index of the Penguin Classics translation, which reads like something out of Jorge Luis Borges: "Cheese, to dream of"; "Clubbing of fingers"; "Goats, liability to epilepsy"; "Women, gout in."

From these texts came medical ideas that persisted well beyond the medieval era: the theory of the four humors (bile, black bile, blood, and phlegm), for instance, comes from the treatise *On the Nature of Man*. The texts are differently shaded as to their opinions, but there is a persistent idea that good health derives from a balance between qualities such as hot and cold, wet and dry. Your geographical position could well affect your health, too: according to the author of *Airs, Waters, Places*, if you are exposed to south winds you can expect moist heads full of phlegm, hemorrhoids and, for women, vaginal discharges. If you are exposed to the north wind, on the other hand, expect constipation, abscesses, and pleurisy . . . and so it cheerfully goes on.

The Hippocratic doctors did not perform dissections on corpses—Aristotle was possibly the first scientist to do this methodically—so, perhaps inevitably, they tended to be rather obsessed by the body's surface: temperature, discharges, urine, mucus, and suchlike. There is also a focus on dietetics that seems entirely familiar to anyone who opens up a newspaper to read about the latest fad for "superfoods" or omega-3. And women's health very much gets its own category, with tremendous interest in menstrual cycles, the womb (always wandering up and down the body, the pesky thing), and pregnancy. There are some rather extraordinary ideas: people who lisp are particularly prone to diarrhea, for instance; sperm originates in the head and passes down through the marrow before exiting via its accustomed route (presumably this made sense because it's all white and slightly gelatinous); the Scythians become impotent because of excessive horse riding. The Corpus is, to say the least, marvelously diverse.

What these texts have in common, though, is the broad notion that disease was naturally explicable, not the result of (say) punishment from angry gods. Occasionally, the doctors refer to incantation or prayer; but this is rare. The author of *On the Sacred Disease* argues his case about epilepsy (presumably against prevailing lay wisdom) thus: "I do not believe that the 'sacred disease' is any more divine or sacred than any other disease but, on the contrary, has specific characteristics and a definite cause . . ." One might, however, point out that the author's "natural" explanation for epilepsy, which relates to internal discharges of phlegm, is just as unevidenced as the claim that the affliction is the gods' work.

Some of the most interesting—and poignant—parts of the Corpus are the several books of *Epidemics*, which are case histories of diseases afflicting individuals. We don't get detailed doctors' notes quite like this again until the nineteenth century. Here's an example (a short one—certain cases are followed for up to forty days):

A woman of the household of Pantimides took a fever the first day after a miscarriage. Tongue was parched; thirst, nausea and insomnia, bowels disordered, the stools being thin, copious and raw.

Second day: rigors, high fever, much purgation; did not sleep.

Third day: pains more intense.

Fourth day: became delirious.

Seventh day: died. The bowels were relaxed throughout, the stools being watery, thin, raw and voluminous; urine thin and little.

Epidemics 3 10
Translation: J. Chadwick and W. N. Mann

Don't say I didn't warn you about the stool-and-urine obsession. Still, what you do get a sense of here is a high level of patient care and careful observation. In fact, the Corpus is fascinating in what it presents about the attitude of doctors to their work, to patients, to medical ethics, and the important question of bedside manner. The author of *Prognosis*, for instance, starts his treatise thus:

> It seems to be highly desirable that a physician should pay much attention to prognosis. If he is able to tell his patients when he visits them not only about their past and present symptoms, but also to tell them what is going to happen, as well as to fill in the details they have omitted, he will increase his reputation as a medical practitioner and people will have no qualms about putting themselves under his care.
>
> *Prognosis* 1
> Translation: J. Chadwick and W. N. Mann

Any doctor will tell you that the patient's confidence in the medical practitioner is absolutely crucial, no less today than it was two and a half thousand years ago. Modern doctors would probably also nod at the good sense of this advice from the author of *Epidemics*:

> Practise two things in your dealings with disease: either help or do not harm the patient. There are three factors in the practice of medicine: the disease, the patient and the physician. The physician is the servant of the science, and the patient must do what he can to fight the disease with the assistance of the physician.
>
> *Epidemics* 1
> Translation: J. Chadwick and W. N. Mann

And then, of course, there is the Hippocratic Oath. My father, a former surgeon, is very fond of telling me how it is a complete canard that doctors swear this oath (although modernized forms of it have been sworn at various times and at various medical schools). Certainly, it wouldn't get us very far today. Nonetheless, as the first statement of ethical standards in medicine, it is a fascinating document, containing the earliest articulation of principles we take for granted, such as patient confidentiality; and with conspicuous mention of still-contentious issues such as abortion.

The real triumph of empiricism, though, was through Aristotle's bafflingly impressive achievements as a thinker and scientist. Aristotle was born in 384 in Stagira in the Chalcidice, the three-pronged peninsula resembling a fork that juts out from Macedonia into the Mediterranean. He came to Athens and was part of Plato's Academy until the great philosopher died in 348. After that, he traveled to Assos on the Turkish coast, just north of the island of Lesbos, accepting an invitation from the tyrant there, Hermias, a former fellow student at the Academy. Here, and later on Lesbos, Aristotle undertook the zoological researches that are among his most impressive achievements. In 342 he became tutor to the future Alexander the Great in Macedon; and subsequently returned to Athens where he set up his own philosophical school, the Lyceum. (The place acquired another name, *peripatos*, from its colonnade; the Aristotelian philosophers are often known as the peripatetics. Our "peripatetic" teachers—ones who travel, or teach at different venues—derive their name from Aristotle's walking up and down the colonnade while he taught.)

Aristotle was a voracious, incredibly ambitious collector of information: on astronomy, meteorology, psychology, even state constitutions. The works we attribute to Aristotle are actually lecture notes taken down by pupils, and the scope is staggering. His most influential contribution to Western thought, of course, was his towering work on logic, metaphysics, and moral philosophy, which continues to set the agenda for philosophers today. As a scientist, his research ranged briskly through what we would now call physics and chemistry—and also, perhaps most impressively of all, biology.

THE HIPPOCRATIC OATH

I swear by Apollo the healer, by Asclepius, by Health and all the powers of healing, and call to witness all the gods and goddesses that I may keep this Oath and Promise to the best of my ability and judgement.

I will pay the same respect to my master in the Science as to my parents and share my life with him and pay all my debts to him. I will regard his sons as my brothers and teach them the Science, if they desire to learn it, without fee or contract. I will hand on precepts, lectures and all other learning to my sons, to those of my master and to those pupils duly apprenticed and sworn, and to none other.

I will use my power to help the sick to the best of my ability and judgement; I will abstain from harming or wronging any man by it.

I will not give a fatal draught to anyone if I am asked, nor will I suggest any such thing. Neither will I give women means to procure an abortion.

I will be chaste in my religious life and in my practice.

I will not cut, even for the stone, but I will leave such procedures to the practitioners of that craft.

Whenever I go into a house, I will go to help the sick and never with the intention of doing harm or injury. I will not abuse my position to indulge in sexual contacts with the bodies of women or of men, whether they be freemen or slaves.

Whatever I see or hear, professionally or privately, which ought not to be divulged, I will keep secret and tell no one.

If, therefore, I observe this Oath and do not violate it, may I prosper both in my life and in my profession, earning good repute among all men for all time. If I transgress and forswear this Oath, may my lot be otherwise.

Translation: J. Chadwick and W. N. Mann

In several books—including *The Inquiry Concerning Animals*, *The Parts of Animals*, and *The Generation of Animals*—Aristotle identified and described around 500 species, including 120 types of fish and around sixty insects. It's an incredible achievement, from a standing start: to be sure, fishermen and hunters would have had a working, practical knowledge of the types of creature they were capturing, but Aristotle was quite simply the first person to attempt to set down, methodically and rationally, their appearance, behavior, habitats, and, using observations gleaned from dissections, anatomy. He described cranes, grebes, and quails; mullet, scorpion fish, and congers; dormice, tortoises, and geckos; crayfish, lobsters, scallops, and crabs. There are sections on the diseases of domesticated mammals (horses, he claims, can miscarry at the smell of a lamp being put out, while elephants are particularly prone to flatulence). He observes that moles occur in Boeotia around Orchomenos, but not in neighboring Lebadeia. He looks at winter plumage and migration, and the nesting habits of the swallow and the cuckoo. Fascinatingly, as we saw in chapter 3, he compares animal habits to human constitutional affairs, describing, in the *Inquiry*, men, bees, wasps, ants, and cranes as *politikoi*, that is, suited to living in a community resembling a Greek *polis*. "Some of them live under a ruler, some have no ruler, ants and innumerable others do not"—just like communities in the Greek world. What makes man different from animals is that man is capable of reason and belief and, though certain animals can memorize skills or repeat speech, like the parrot, only man can recall at will, he says.

There are, let it be said, a great number of errors in Aristotle's books. For instance, in the *Inquiry*, there is a hilarious passage that describes how bison, when hunted, attack the dogs pursuing them with bursts of projectile, abrasive dung. Perhaps some old hunter was having the poor fellow on. One also looks askance at the way he uses arguments from nature to support the idea of the inferiority of women (men are still at this particular game, of course). "The male," he writes, ". . . is a readier ally and braver than the female, since among the cephalopods, when the cuttlefish has been struck by the trident, the male comes to the female's help, whereas the female runs away when the male has been struck." Thanks, Aristotle.

Equally, there are observations that were for many centuries mistrusted, and later—often quite recently—found to have been correct. For instance, he describes a particular kind of viviparous dogfish that reproduces by way of an embryo attached by an umbilical-cord-like string to a placenta-like structure in the womb. Eyebrows were raised up until 1842, when Johannes Müller, the German ichthyologist (the word is derived from the Greek *ichthus*, meaning "fish") showed that Aristotle had got it right all along. In all important essentials, Aristotle's *Inquiry* is amazingly percipient and all-embracing—and rather a wonderful read.

Perhaps the most important thing about Greek science was the way it was connected to the tides of Greek intellectual revolution as a whole. Our first scientist-philosopher, Thales, was a contemporary of Solon of Athens, who famously reformed the city's law code and displayed it, for all to see, inscribed in public on wooden pillars. The scientists of ancient Greece were operating in this spirit: one of open discussion, where knowledge and intellectual development were valued in themselves. An ambitious worldview could be formulated, and then debated, perhaps rejected, perhaps developed. Questions were not there to be closed down, but opened up, turned on their heads, examined from every angle. The scientists' undimmed intellectual energy, their bracing curiosity about the world, laid the foundations of Enlightenment thinking—and are qualities of which we seem now to have greater need by the day.

8. The death of Socrates and the birth of philosophy:
The challenge of Plato's *Republic*

THE BIRTH OF Western philosophy began with a death: the execution of Socrates in 399. This event has been seen as an almost Christlike martyrdom—an heroic self-sacrifice in the face of an ignorant, brutal authority. In fact, early Christians were happy to reel him in as an honorary colleague, someone who was prevented from seeing the light only by his dying 400 years too soon. In his long and eventful afterlife, Socrates has also been reincarnated as political martyr, doughty thinker, and upholder of free speech and rational dissent—a view sustained by philosophers, activists, and artists such as John Stuart Mill, Martin Luther King, and David (in his masterful 1787 painting *The Death of Socrates*).

But Socrates' execution also remains a deeply traumatic subject. It's easier to mourn his death if you are an anti-democrat, if you believe (as was the broad consensus in modern political thought until at least the mid-nineteenth century), that ancient democracy represented the worst excesses of mob rule. But his death is a real problem if you do believe in democracy. How did the Athenians, champions of freedom and equality, come to execute their most important thinker? Could a democracy really allow a seventy-year-old man to be killed, a man who, you might say, never did any harm to anyone, but simply wandered around Athens talking to people? Or were the Athenians right to kill Socrates? Did he, in fact, present an urgent threat to democracy? These questions seem to present themselves with particular urgency now, as modern democratic freedoms appear more and more strained.

Socrates is an enigma because, despite being regarded as the fountainhead of philosophy, he wrote nothing down, gave no public lectures, did not found a school. He was born in 470 or 469, reputedly the son of a stonemason. He had a wife, Xanthippe, and three sons. He did not pursue a trade and was uninterested in acquiring money, instead spending much of his adult life talking and thinking, often accompanied by an entourage of admiring young men. He was charged, in 399, with failing to respect or worship the city's gods; introducing new gods; and corrupting the young (the precise meaning and nature of the charges remain controversial among scholars). He was condemned to death; and had it not been for the influence of his wealthy friends, his execution would have been rather less dignified than his quiet hemlock-aided exit. The garden-variety method in Athens was to be strapped to a wooden board with a metal collar around your neck that would be gradually tightened, strangling you to death.

So we have no account of Socrates in his own words. All we have are versions of the man supplied by other people. Dating from Socrates' lifetime is Aristophanes' comedy *The Clouds*, first produced in 423, which has the philosopher riding around in a basket in the sky communing with his favored deities, the clouds. He teaches the hero Strepsiades how to evade his creditors by making the weaker argument appear the stronger, encourages him to abandon the traditional gods, and finally induces Strepsiades' son Pheidippides to beat his parents—a picture that suggests that at least some Athenians saw Socrates as a pernicious influence. The writer Xenophon also left memoirs of Socrates; but it is Socrates' pupil Plato (c. 427–347) to whom we owe the most extensive picture of the man, including the memorable and moving account of his death in *Phaedo* (see page 144).

In Plato's philosophical works, which are nearly all presented in the form of dialogues, Socrates is omnipresent: talking, teasing out arguments, questioning his friends, chasing—to quote Virginia Woolf—"the dwindling and changing of opinion as it hardens and intensifies into truth." You might even imagine that there was, in Plato's obsessive reimagining of his dead teacher, a traumatized attempt to conjure Socrates back into existence, to rub out the ugly fact of his state-ordered death.

How far Plato accurately represents his hero is open to debate. His first works were not written until well after Socrates' death; it is unclear how far he relies on memory, notes, imaginative reconstruction, or just sheer invention. The "Socrates" of the dialogues seems to vary in character from work to work. Some scholars have been tempted to regard the earlier dialogues, such as *Apology* (an account of Socrates' trial and not an "apology" at all in the normal English sense), as more authentically "Socratic"; and the later works, such as *Republic*, more "Platonic," as the character "Socrates" came simply to be used as a vehicle to carry Plato's own thoughts. Some scholars have even seen Plato as the betrayer of the ideas of Socrates. The great historian George Grote, in his *Plato and the Other Companions of Sokrates* (1865), wrote:

In the Platonic *Apology*, we find Sokrates confessing his own ignorance . . . But the *Republic* presents him in a new character. He is no longer a dissenter amidst a community of fixed, inherited convictions. He is himself in the throne of King Nomos: the infallible authority, temporal as well as spiritual, from whom all public sentiment emanates, and by whom orthodoxy is determined . . . Neither the Sokrates of the Platonic *Apology*, nor his negative dialectic, could be allowed to exist in the Platonic Republic.

We will return to *Republic* later. What was the nature of Socrates' intellectual project? In the *Apology*, Plato has him describing his life of inquiry to the jury. It all started, he said, when his friend Chaerephon asked the Delphic Oracle whether there was anyone wiser than Socrates. The oracle answered that there was not. Interested, Socrates decided to put this to the test, and went to visit a man with a great reputation for wisdom:

> Well, I gave a thorough examination to this person . . . and in conversation with him I formed the impression that although in many people's opinion, and especially in his own, he appeared to be wise, in fact he was not. Then when I began to try to show him that he only thought he was wise and was not really so, my efforts were resented both by him and by many of the other people present. However, I reflected as I walked away: "Well, I am certainly wiser than this man. It is only too likely that neither of us has any knowledge to boast of; but he thinks that he knows something which he does not know, whereas I am quite conscious of my ignorance."

> *Apology* 21c–d
> Translation: Hugh Tredennick and Harold Tarrant

Aiming to do the job thoroughly, Socrates then set about questioning every other class of person he could find, from other supposed wise men to poets, playwrights, and artisans. His conclusion in each case was the same: that none of them was really wise. Perhaps one can see that, while it would be entertaining and useful work to establish the ignorance of the average politician, the Socratic project of proving that everyone in Athens was rather stupid might have begun to grate on the populace after a while. Another example of what the scholar Emily Wilson calls Socrates' "impenitent smugness" can be seen later on in his trial, again according to Plato's *Apology*. Having been found guilty, he is asked to suggest an alternative to the death penalty. In a manner most unhumble, Socrates claims that what he really deserves is a reward: free meals for life in the Prytaneum, an honor generally reserved for great victors in the Olympic Games. You can see how that kind of attitude would simply rub people up the wrong way. Indeed, more jurors voted for his death penalty in this second round of voting than had for his original guilty verdict.

THE DEATH OF SOCRATES

Up till this time most of us had been fairly successful in keeping back our tears; but when we saw that he was drinking, that he had actually drunk it, we could do so no longer; in spite of myself the tears came pouring out, so that I covered my face and wept broken-heartedly—not for him, but for my own calamity in losing such a friend. Crito had given up even before me, and had gone out when he could not restrain his tears. But Apollodorus, who had never stopped crying even before, now broke out into such a storm of passionate weeping that he made everyone in the room break down, except Socrates himself, who said: "Really, my friends, what a way to behave! Why, that was my main reason for sending away the women, to prevent this sort of discordant behaviour; because I am told that one should make one's end in a reverent silence. Calm yourselves and be brave."

This made us feel ashamed, and we controlled our tears. Socrates walked about, and presently, saying that his legs were heavy, lay down on his back—that was what the man recommended. The man (he was the same one who had administered the poison) kept his hand upon Socrates, and after a little while examined his feet and legs; then pinched his foot hard and asked if he felt it. Socrates said no. Then he did the same to his legs; and moving gradually upwards in this way let us see that he was getting cold and numb. Presently he felt him again and said that when it reached the heart, Socrates would be gone.

The coldness was spreading about as far as his waist when Socrates uncovered his face—for he had covered it up—and said (they were his last words): "Crito, we ought to offer a cock to Asclepius. See to it, and don't forget."

"No, it shall be done," said Crito. "Are you sure that there is nothing else?"

Socrates made no reply to this question, but after a little while he stirred; and when the man uncovered him, his eyes were fixed. When Crito saw this, he closed the mouth and eyes.

This, Echecrates, was the end of our comrade, who was, we may fairly say, of all those whom we knew in our time the bravest and also the wisest and most just."

Phaedo 117d–end.
Translation: Hugh Tredennick and Harold Tarrant

Surely Socrates did not die simply for annoying people? What of the charges about failing to respect/worship the traditional gods and bringing in new gods? It is true that Socrates talks a great deal of something called his *daimonion*—a personal deity who he said guided his decisions. This notion, which sounds rather monotheistic, endeared him to the early Christians; and of course, it is very far from a "traditional" god in the Athenian sense, where religion was bound up with civic collectivism rather than with having a relationship, as it were, with a personal god. Nonetheless, the charge seems peculiar in that the Athenians by and large seemed content to tolerate the introduction of new gods—such as, for example, Asclepius, whose cult was adopted in Athens in about 500.

It may help to put these religious concerns into the Athenian cultural context. The fifth century intellectual revolution saw a number of thinkers known as sophists converge on Athens, many of whom went into business teaching wealthy young men philosophy, science, and rhetoric—the last a particularly important art in the city's freshly minted democracy. In Aristophanes' *Clouds*, it seems to be Socrates the sophist who is being pilloried, Socrates the newfangled thinker who could make the weaker argument win out over the stronger. (By extension, one can imagine the anxieties that might have been aroused by the spectacle of highly educated, well-born young men swaying opinion in the Assembly by means of their expert speaking.) The sophists' scientific thinking also saw them begin to take a more rational approach to phenomena in the physical world, putting them down to naturally explicable causes rather than to the gods, as we saw in chapter 7. Socrates claimed he was not a sophist: he had nothing to teach, he said, and unlike the sophists did not charge his young associates. But surely to most people he would have looked like one; and he may, to an extent, have been paying the price of a popular suspicion towards this breed of novel thinkers.

In the end, though, the charge that assumes most importance is that of corrupting young men. When the Athenians finally and disastrously lost the Peloponnesian War in 404, democracy was overthrown by a group called the Thirty Tyrants. A grotesque reign of terror ensued, during which 1,500 Athenians were killed. Quite quickly, the democracy was restored, but the defeat by the Spartans and the ravages wrought by the Thirty Tyrants left Athens a wrecked and bloody place. One of these tyrants was Critias, Plato's uncle—who had been taught by Socrates. A speech, written half a century later by the orator Aeschines, gives us the following as a scrap of evidence: "Men of Athens, you executed Socrates the sophist because he was clearly responsible for the education of Critias, one of the thirty anti-democratic leaders." It is circumstantial, but it gives us a hint that the restored democracy may have turned on the irritant Socrates as a scapegoat.

You can hold Socrates' death up to the light and see it in any number of ways: as a reasonable way of dealing with a dangerous anti-democrat, perhaps (particularly bearing in mind he could almost certainly have avoided the death penalty had he accepted his friends' help to spirit him out of Athens). Or you could see it as the judicial murder of a hero who stood for free speech and freethinking against a repressive, ignorant majority. Or you could even find it a plain old cock-up, the kind of miscarriage of justice that simply happens in the real world, even in basically fair political setups. Plato's response, it seems, was doggedly and persistently to pursue philosophy, to scratch away at the questions left hanging by Socrates and by Socrates' death: What is the good life? What is virtue? And, perhaps most importantly: what is justice?

Plato's *Republic*—the most famous work by arguably the most important philosopher the West has produced—is an answer to the last question. To me, it is bloated, uneven, chilling, funny, exasperating, beautiful, inspiring, deadly, and confusing. Most importantly, it is a gauntlet thrown down and a challenge issued: a challenge to think, a challenge to engage and to argue. It seems a shame to me that *Republic* is universally known of but little read: no one said that following Plato's arguments was an easygoing exercise, but the shock and breathtaking ambition of *Republic* make it an absolute page-turner. *Republic* is the original utopian text, the precursor to Thomas More's *Utopia* and Samuel Butler's *Erewhon*; but it is also the great-granddaddy of dystopian books from George Orwell's *1984* to Margaret Atwood's *The Handmaid's Tale* (sharing with the latter an interest in the politics of procreation). Karl Popper, in his 1945 work *The Open Society and Its Enemies*, characterised Plato's *Republic* as the mother of all totalitarian states. George Grote claimed that a dissenting mind like Socrates could never have existed in Plato's *Republic* (see above). On the other hand, it is plausibly the one state where Socrates could not have been put to death: this hypothetical *polis*, after all, is to be ruled by philosopher-kings.

So what is Plato's *Republic*? First, to clear up one potential mis-understanding: *Republic* has nothing to do with proposing a repub-lican system of government. In Greek, its title is *Politeia*, which is one of those difficult-to-translate words: you might try polity, or constitution—but these are approximations. The usual Latin trans-lation of the word is *res publica*, another tricky phrase—it means pub-lic affairs, politics. But *res publica* gives us the English word republic, and *Republic*, as the title of the work, is what we are stuck with.

Republic, like nearly all Plato's works, is presented in dialogue form, and it starts with a lengthy, vivid, conversational stage-setter. (Plato "had the dramatic genius," as Virginia Woolf said.) Socrates is with his friend Glaucon attending a sacrifice at Piraeus. On their way back to Athens, they are waylaid and invited to the house of the wealthy Cephalus and his sons Polemarchus and Lysias; Thra-symachus the sophist is also in attendance. Conversation turns to the nature of justice (in Greek, *dikaiosune*, often translated as moral-ity; we must think of "justice" in this context as a very broad term). Thrasymachus claims that a life of injustice is more worthwhile and profitable than one of justice. (As in "The rain it raineth on the just / But also on the unjust fellow / But mostly on the just / Because the unjust steals the just's umbrella.") Cephalus suggests justice is about basic precepts such as not lying or stealing; though as conversation becomes more intense and detailed, he slips out of the conversation. Polemarchus suggests that justice is "giving everyone what they are owed"; Socrates deflects this by suggesting that Polemarchus con-ceives of justice as a mere technical skill, as it were, rather than re-lated on a deeper level to the state of the soul. Thrasymachus argues that justice is about "might is right" (the sort of thing that would have appealed to the Athenians of Thucydides' Melian Dialogue; see chapter 5). Glaucon challenges Socrates to argue that injustice would not be worthwhile even if you were guaranteed to get away with unjust acts—if, for example, you owned a ring of invisibility such that your peccadilloes were bound never to be discovered. Socrates contends that it is worth being just for its own sake *and* because it has good consequences for the individual. Being just, he says, leads to happiness. He undertakes to answer the challenge by presenting an extraordinarily broad, deep, ambitious (and often perilously indirect) answer to the question—via the imaginative creation of an ideal state.

The republic (let's use that shorthand) of *Republic* starts off with Socrates building up a hypothetical community from the barest bones, and thinking about how each member could best contribute to the whole. The dialogue quickly establishes that each person will do "their own thing." But that doesn't mean that citizens are expected freely to mind their own business; rather, chillingly, that the man who is best suited to being a cobbler will always devote himself to shoemaking, the man best suited to being a doctor will always devote himself to medicine, and so on. There is nothing here, in other words, to recognize individual desires or personal freedom. In fact, the cobbler who fancies doing a bit of farming will be prevented from so doing: no room for dilettantes in the republic. Even more unsettlingly, Socrates argues that if a carpenter, say, develops a chronic disease that prevents him from fulfilling his role as a carpenter, his life is not worth living; it would simply be better if he were dead. This is also, grotesquely, a republic in which disabled children are to be exposed; for no one can "practice virtue" who cannot lead a normally healthy life.

Who will protect and keep the the community safe? Socrates puts forward the idea of guardians, who "will have a philosopher's love of knowledge." These guardians (the "philosopher-kings") are the best and brightest of the city, the elite; the class divisions between them and the other inhabitants are absolute. They will explain these class divisions to the rest of the populace by feeding them the myth that some people have gold in their souls, others silver, others bronze, others iron. (This is an adaptation of the myth of ages in Hesiod's *Works and Days*.) Plato, then, is happy for his rulers to lie to the people—a curious position, you might say, for someone who was so keen on the search for truth. Later, we learn more about the guardians: they are to have no private property; and their children are to be brought up communally, by the state. Staggeringly, Socrates suggests that women might too become guardians, that there is no innate reason to prevent them from becoming rulers on a par (or almost on a par) with men. It is hard to imagine just how insanely provocative this suggestion would have seemed in the fourth century BC (and of course continued to seem well into the twentieth century AD). Plato may as well have suggested that pigs could become philosopher-kings.

The question of the education of these guardians is of vital importance to Plato: they are to be the backbone of a perfectly just state, after all. *Republic*'s foray into educational theory has been deeply influential, in that it regards education as the formation of character rather than simply the acquisition of skills—and is also notorious, because of Socrates' attack on the arts, an attack that will become yet more extreme at the end of the book.

What Plato explores here is the effects of poetry. Having established that what's wrong with Homer is that he portrays heroes and gods not as exemplars, but as liars, objects of ridicule, or emotional wrecks, he launches an attack on "imitation"—the effects not of poetry in itself but of, as it were, direct speech in poetry. This of course encompasses drama *tout court*. The idea is that an actor might be adversely affected by taking on the role of an evil individual. On the face of it, this looks absurd. True, there are extreme cases of actors having become very deeply wrapped up in their parts: Daniel Day-Lewis was so subsumed by the role of Hamlet that he believed that he was talking to the ghost of his own father, the poet Cecil Day-Lewis, as he acted; and Forest Whitaker inhabited his Oscar-winning role as Idi Amin in *The Last King of Scotland* so fully that at least one other cast member became fearful of this normally genial fellow, even when the cameras were not rolling. But there are (mercifully) no reports of these two fine actors assuming the characteristics of Hamlet or Idi Amin in the long term. Nor do actors, as far as we know, follow the Method so surely that they murder and steal to prepare for their roles as murderers and thieves. But before we write the thought off, we also have to remember that ancient Greece was not a reading culture but, largely, an oral culture; that education was clustered around the great texts of Homer, which would be learned and recited; and that great parts of Homer are in direct speech (he is, as Plato rightly says, the "original tragedian"). So acting out roles would have been much more familiar to educated Greeks; where we read silently in our heads, the Greeks would have been reciting out loud. We also might be reminded of the fact that there is, in our own culture, a continuing debate about, for instance, whether children imitate things they have seen in violent films, or whether rap music contributes to gun culture. Art is not necessarily all about the useful and positive increase of empathy: we might well argue that some art is indeed pernicious.

At the end of *Republic*, the view towards the arts hardens. The early section on education ruled out only "imitative" poetry and certain kinds of music (the exception being music written in the rousing, militaristic Dorian and Phrygian modes). At the close of the work, Plato launches a jeremiad on painting, and on poetry itself—a sort of love-hate attack in which he banishes poetry entirely from the putative state. Of Homer he says, "We'll do what a lover does when he thinks that a love affair he is involved in is no good for him: he reluctantly detaches himself." It is paradoxical to say the least that in *Republic* Plato uses literary tools to condemn literature. *Republic* is a work conveyed in dialogue form (direct speech!) and in lucid, flowing language. It frequently quotes poets, including Aeschylus and

Homer himself, and employs vivid poetic imagery. There's a wonderful simile in which Socrates likens the soul in the human body, tainted by its bodily association, to the sea god Glaucus' body, which is covered in shells and weed. Oddly, even though there are so many ugly notes in *Republic*, it is this reluctant banishment of poetry that I find particularly grueling and upsetting. This is a state that will admit only of "hymns to the gods and eulogies of virtuous men." Terrifying.

Both grotesque and wonderful: this is how Plato's *Republic* seems to me. At the heart of the book come the three famous analogies: the Sun, the Line, and the Cave. The analogy of the Sun is meant to illustrate the supreme importance of the philosophical study of the Form of Good for the guardians. We have stumbled here into Plato's "theory" of Forms. (And it is important to realize that this is never a theory worked out and presented in full, but a shifting set of ideas that comes into play in different ways in different Platonic dialogues.) To put this delicate idea utterly crudely, the general idea is that an ideal "Form" of qualities (or sometimes objects) exists, as it were, in a realm that can be reached only by pure intellect and not by the senses. In this central part of the *Republic*, the notion is that any particular instance of beauty, smallness, bigness, or justice could also, in a different context, be taken as an instance of its opposite. So you could decide that Matthew, at six feet two inches, is tall—until you happened to compare him to the Statue of Liberty, when you would have to concede that he is small. To make sense of the terms big, small, etc., one thus conceives of an absolute quality that is bigness or smallness itself—a Form of bigness or smallness—that does not contain its opposite, and therefore must exist outside the physical world. (You will note that this runs into trouble for terms that do not have an opposite, though later in *Republic* Plato does talk of objects such as tables relating to an ideal Form.)

So, to turn back to the analogy of the Sun: Socrates says that the sun in the visible world is like the Good in the realm of thought. As the sun allows objects to be seen by the eye, so the Good allows objects of knowledge to be known by the mind. Now, it's fantastically unclear how the Good performs this particular role, but it's a truly inspiring passage: a call to arms for the intellect. Passing swiftly over the rather difficult analogy of the Line, which sets up a sort of hierarchy of knowledge and belief (with intellectual grasp of the Forms at the top) in geometrical form, now comes the analogy of the Cave.

This is surely one of Plato's most magnificent and influential literary creations. Here's how it begins:

"Next," [Socrates] said, "here's a situation which you can use as an analogy for the human condition—for our education or lack of it. Imagine people living in a cavernous cell down under the ground; at the far end of the cave, a long way off, there's an entrance open to the outside world. They've been there since childhood, with their legs and necks tied up in a way which keeps them in one place and allows them to look only straight ahead, but not to turn their heads. There's firelight burning a long way further up the cave behind them, and up the slope between the fire and the prisoners there's a road, beside which you should imagine a low wall has been built—like the partition which conjurors place between themselves and their audience and above which they show their tricks."

"All right," [Glaucon] said.

"Imagine also that there are people on the other side of this wall who are carrying all sorts of artefacts. These artefacts, human statuettes, and animal models carved in stone and wood and all kinds of materials stick out over the wall; and as you'd expect, some of the people talk as they carry these objects along, while others are silent."

Republic 514a–515a.
Translation: Robin Waterfield

If you imagine this as a picture for a moment (an exceptionally strange and beautiful picture) you can see what Socrates is getting at. The prisoners' only view of the world is the flickering shadows of the statuettes cast by the flames; a sort of meaningless, narrativeless Indonesian shadow play. (The prisoners see the world, you might say, "through a glass darkly.") Socrates now asks Glaucon to imagine what would happen if one of the prisoners were to escape from the cave—and see the visible world as it really is. The shock and revelation of this vision would be, says Socrates, like the mind's ascent to the realm of the Forms. What Plato presents is the most moving image of the excitement of philosophical inquiry, of the possibility of the mind casting off the fetters of conventional thinking to strike forth for enlightenment and truth. (It has also had, of course, enormous influence—to cite just one example, the very fine film *The Matrix* is a reimagining of the analogy of the Cave, with the hero Neo, played by Keanu Reeves, breaking free of the world of shadow play (the "matrix") to achieve insight of the true nature of things.)

I haven't even begun (and nor do I propose) to engage with the nitty-gritty of Plato's arguments about the nature of knowledge, the tripartite division of the mind and so on. What I have wanted to suggest is the shocking, paradoxical nature of *Republic*, and why it begs to be read, in all its ugliness and beauty. I can't help tending to the view that this city of Plato's, if made real, would be a place of nightmares beyond imagining. But what saves it, for me, is that it is not (surely) a blueprint for a "real" state. Plato is not setting out a law code or phrasing a constitution. The *Republic* is provisional, it is a thinking-out-loud. It is important that it is not a treatise: it is a dialogue. As we read this work, with its to-and-fro talk, we are surely encouraged to weigh in, to take part in this conversation, to become one of Socrates' less pliable interlocutors. In short, to argue back. It is a call to arms. One of the most telling details in *Republic* for me is what happens to Cephalus. Having offered some not-very-intelligent, conventional ideas about the nature of justice at the beginning of the work, he disappears from the conversation, saying that he must "attend the sacrifice" (which in itself sounds like a ropey excuse—the religious festival Socrates has been attending is, we are told, over). I have a nasty feeling that I would be the Cephalus in this conversation: too lazy to engage, too complacent to question accepted beliefs, too pliable to answer back. The question is, can any of us afford to be a Cephalus? Are we really safe, now as in the fourth century, to take the nature of justice and morality for granted?

9. Love and loss:
Desire in Homer, Sappho, and Plato

LOVE SURROUNDS US. Eros, who steals your wits away and sends you silly with desire, is the oldest of the gods, the reason anything exists at all. But Eros is also a child, and a naughty child at that, bow and arrow in hand, attendant and partner-in-crime of mighty Aphrodite. A fragment from Sappho, that great writer on love and longing, reads:

> Like a down-rushing whirlwind flying at an oak-tree, Eros has shaken my heart . . .

Eros is elemental and unreasoning; even doughty oaks are no proof against it. Eros is (in another Sapphic fragment) bittersweet, irresistible, can't be fought off.

The gods in the ancient Greek world love magnificently and abundantly. Despite the presence of a formidable, jealous wife, Zeus is always falling for others—goddesses, women, and young men (such as Ganymede, a mortal snatched up to Mount Olympus to be the gods' cupbearer at feasts). Zeus loved Danaë, who was kept in seclusion by her father, a princess in a tower. The god impregnated her disguised as a shower of gold: the result of that (deities always being super-fertile) was the hero Perseus, the one who lopped off Medusa's head. Zeus also loved Semele, a princess of Thebes, who stupidly asked to see him undisguised in his naked reality as the king of the gods. The thunderbolt power of him burned her up, but their son, the god Dionysus, survived. Zeus seduced Alcmena disguised as her own husband, and their child was Heracles. As a swan Zeus made love to Leda, who gave birth to the jaw-dropping beauty Helen, as well as Clytemnestra, Castor, and Polydeuces—a lost but copied painting by Leonardo has Leda's children popping out of giant-sized eggs while the proud father, long white neck hung around with garlands of flowers, nuzzles against his girlfriend.

The gods have affairs among themselves, too: Aphrodite and the war god Ares were besotted with each other, despite the fact that she was married to the lame Hephaestus, the Olympians' most prodigiously talented craftsman. The story is told in the *Odyssey*, one of the bard Demodocus' songs in Book 8. Helios, the sun god, found out about the affair and told Hephaestus, who constructed a trap: a beautifully wrought net of fantastically fine gold chain, invisible to the naked eye, even to a god's eye, which he hung over Aphrodite's bed. Hephaestus pretended to go off to his favorite island, Lemnos, but quietly turned back when Helios tipped him the wink: sure enough, Ares had not wasted the opportunity for an afternoon of love, and now the pair were inescapably trapped by the net of precious tracery. All the gods gathered to make fun of the guilty couple, and to laugh at the wretchedly furious Hephaestus. Aphrodite and Ares in love was an idea transformed in Renaissance art into the idea of Mars disarmed—war subdued by love—like Botticelli's *Venus and Mars* in the National Gallery in London.

The way Homer talked about love stamps down a standard for those who followed: the way he deals with desire and affection is still as percipient, funny, and poignant as anything written since. In the center of the *Iliad*, Book 14, is another wonderful love scene between two gods: this time it's a seduction, not without its humorous moments, by Hera of her husband Zeus. She wants to lure him into a postcoital slumber so that she can have her own way for a while on the battlefield, and give the Greeks a helping hand. So as to look her best (see chapter 4) she borrows Aphrodite's magic breastband, woven through with Love and Longing. She then speeds off to Mount Ida, near Troy, where Zeus is stationed, meekly pretending she's just dropped by to ask his permission to visit the seabed to mediate in a row between Ocean and his wife Tethys. (A likely story! As if Hera ever asked anyone's permission for anything.) Desire washes over Zeus—"I've never been so overwhelmed, Hera, not even when I made love to Danaë or Semele or Alcmena," he tells her.

> With that the son of Cronus caught his wife in his arms
> and under them now the holy earth burst with fresh green grass,
> crocus and hyacinth, clover soaked with dew, so thick and soft
> it lifted their bodies off the hard, packed ground . . .
> Folded deep in that bed they lay and round them wrapped
> a marvellous cloud of gold, and glistening showers of dew
> rained down around them both.
>
> *Iliad* 14 413–418

I love the idea of flowers springing forth where they make love . . . a pathetic fallacy *avant la lettre*. The hyacinth was born out of love, albeit of the doomed variety, in the first place: the god Apollo loved the young man Hyacinthus, and one day they were competing at discus together. Apollo threw with the tremendous strength of a god; some say the discus was blown off course by Zephyrus, the west wind, who was jealous. Anyway, whatever the cause, that discus flew straight at Hyacinthus and killed him. Hyacinths sprang up from the drops of blood, each petal marked with a *Y*, in Greek the first letter of his name (with a squint and a bit of imagination, you can still see it). And when Athena gives Odysseus the ultimate makeover to prepare him for the climactic moment when he will reveal himself to Penelope in the *Odyssey*, the goddess makes his hair gleam and curl like bunches of the rich, fragrant, heady flower.

One of the ways of looking at the *Odyssey*'s architecture is to think of it as the hero's progression through various different kinds of encounter with women, building up to his final showdown, then loving reunion, with his true soulmate, Penelope. At the beginning of the poem, we're told he is longing for his home and his wife, but Calypso the nymph is holding him back, keeping him captive on her island, making him share her bed. When Hermes arrives to tell her it's time for the wanderer to go, she even offers Odysseus immortality, but he, a man who always has the right thing to say, offers the nymph the most tactful of rejections:

> "Ah great goddess,"
> worldly Odysseus answered, "don't be angry with me,
> please. All that you say is true, how well I know.
> Look at my wise Penelope. She falls far short of you,
> your beauty, stature. She is mortal after all
> and you, you never age or die . . .
> Nevertheless I long—I pine, all my days—
> to travel home and see the dawn of my return."
>
> *Odyssey* 5 236–243.

Odysseus also has a romantic brush with Circe the witch, who, once he has managed to prevent her from turning him into a pig, becomes a rather more sympathetic proposition, a generous host and resourceful ally who doesn't complain when Odysseus and his men take their leave (see chapter 6); and then there's Nausicaa . . .

When Odysseus leaves Calypso's island on a homemade raft, his exit does not escape the angry attention of Poseidon, who sends a terrible storm that thrashes and lashes the hero half to death. He washes up on the shore of a mysterious island, the land of the Phaeacians. Exhausted, he finds a place to sleep under an olive tree. Meanwhile, Athena visits the bedroom of the island's princess, and sends her a broad hint in a dream: she should get up the next morning and wash her beautiful dresses, you never know, her wedding day might not be so far off, and she'll need to have her trousseau all spick and span.

Accordingly, the next morning, Nausicaa and her maids go down to the river to wash the princess's clothes. At noon, they stop and spread the gorgeous fabrics out over the riverbank to dry. They begin to play a game of ball. One of them throws it right into the scrub, and it wakes up Odysseus who, massive, unkempt, salt-caked and . . . naked, crawls out of the bushes, a branch discreetly deployed before his groin. The girls scream and scatter—all except Nausicaa, who, with a breath of courage sent her by Athena, stands her ground. Odysseus toys with the idea of clasping her knees, the standard gesture of supplication, but discards it: he'd scare the wits out of the poor girl. Instead, he keeps his distance and constructs a typically winning speech, more than a little flirtatious: the man who takes you home as a bride, he says, will be the luckiest fellow alive.

Nausicaa takes pity on him and promises him help. Odysseus bathes in the river, rubs himself down with oil, and puts on some clothes that Nausicaa lends him. Athena does her special thing, and, like a master craftsman putting the final touches to a exquisite object, makes him look absolutely breathtaking. "If only a man like that were my husband," thinks Nausicaa. It's a wonderfully moving picture—you know Odysseus isn't going to marry Nausicaa, or even that she's anything but momentarily smitten, but there's a sort of delicate understanding between them, an understated delight: the young girl and the hardened but splendidly built warrior. Nausicaa advises Odysseus how to approach her royal parents, who (formidable as they are) help him out and fix him up with a boat to Ithaca. Nausicaa fades from the story, except there's a terrific moment when, just as Odysseus has stepped out of the bath and dressed for dinner, she appears from behind a column and accosts him—remember me, she says, when you reach your home: you owe your life to me. I'll remember you, he answers, for the rest of my life, I'll worship you as a goddess . . .

The book's great marriage of true minds, however, is that between Odysseus and Penelope, perhaps one of the great sympathetic and equal relationships in literature. When Penelope has finally recognized her long-lost husband—one of the most moving scenes in Homer, if not literature full stop (see chapter 4) they go to bed together:

> But the royal couple, once they'd revelled in all
> the longed-for joys of love, revelled in each other's stories,
> the radiant woman telling of all she'd borne at home,
> watching them there, the infernal crowd of suitors
> slaughtering herds of cattle and good fat sheep—
> while keen to win her hand—
> draining the broached vats dry of vintage wine.
> And great Odysseus told his wife of all the pains
> he had dealt out to other men and all the hardships
> he'd endured himself—his story first to last—
> and she listened on, enchanted . . .
> Sleep never sealed her eyes till all was told.
>
> *Odyssey* 23 342–353

They rejoice in each other; their adventures, hers at home and his far away, are made equal.

Love completed and requited: the *Odyssey* has its fairytale ending. The *Iliad*, however, is a darker, some would say richer business, also suffused with love, but a love that is cut through with loss. It's not a simple picture: in the *Iliad* we are often dealing with, as it were, anticipated loss, a loss that is more infinitely poignant because the characters do not yet even know about it. In Book 3, Helen stands on Troy's ramparts with Priam, pointing out the Greek champions to him. She picks out all the great leaders, but wonders where her brothers, Castor and Polydeuces are:

> "Perhaps
> they never crossed over from Lacedaemon's lovely hills
> or come they did, sailing here in the deep-sea ships,
> but now they refuse to join the men in battle,
> dreading the scorn, the curses hurled at me . . ."
> So she wavered, but the earth already held them fast,
> long dead in the life-giving earth of Lacedaemon,
> the dear land of their fathers.
>
> *Iliad* 3 283–290

It's like the devastating moment at the end of chapter 32 of Thackeray's *Vanity Fair*, the aftermath of the battle of Waterloo—"Darkness came down on the field and city: and Amelia was praying for George, who was lying on his face, dead, with a bullet through his heart."

The love between Hector, prince of Troy, and his wife Andromache provides the poem with its emotional heart, giving this tale of fighting men a depth that goes beyond the battlefield. I don't think I'm physically capable of reading *Iliad* Book 6 without weeping. This is where Andromache meets her husband by the Scaean gate of Troy, with their tiny child, Astyanax. She pleads with Hector to take a defensive stand near the city rather than heading out to face the risks of the battlefield. She reminds him of her terrible past: her father and brothers were butchered by Achilles when he sacked her home city; her mother was enslaved and ransomed, but then shot down and killed by one of Artemis' deadly arrows. Andromache says (this for me is the dissolution point, even as I write):

> "You, Hector—you are my father now, my noble mother, a brother too, and you are my husband, young, and warm and strong!"
>
> Iliad 6 509–510

He must go out and fight, he says, despite his pity for her . . . even so, he says, the pain of the prospect of the death of his brothers, even of his mother and father, is nothing to him,

> ". . . beside your agony
> when some brazen Argive hales you off in tears,
> wrenching away your day of light and freedom!
> Then far off in the land of Argos you must live,
> labouring at a loom, at another's beck and call
> fetching water at some spring, Messeis or Hyperia,
> resisting it all the way—
> the rough yoke of necessity at your neck.
> And a man may say, who sees your streaming tears,
> 'There is the wife of Hector, the bravest fighter
> they could field, those stallion-breaking Trojans,
> long ago when the men fought for Troy.' So he will say
> and the fresh grief will swell your heart once more,
> widowed, robbed of the one man strong enough
> to fight off your day of slavery.
> No, no,
> let the earth come piling over my dead body
> before I hear your cries, I hear you dragged away!"
>
> Iliad 6 539–555

All the more poignant because, as Homer's original audience would surely have known, this prefigures precisely what does happen. Hector will die too soon to protect her; Troy will fall. The story of what happened next to Andromache is indeed told in Euripides' bleak play *Trojan Women*, in which a particularly terrible slaughter is reserved for the baby Astyanax whose very name, "lord of the city," is a cruel irony (see chapter 5).

Hector now bends to kiss his son—who cries out and weeps, frightened by his father's plumed helmet. The hero and his wife laugh, and Hector pulls off the helmet, and picks up his son. (How many soldiers since must have had similar encounters? It makes me think of men returning from wars to children who barely know them.) But they are smiling through tears. Later, Hector's mother, Hecuba, hears the news of her son's death.

> Her voice rang out in tears, but the wife of Hector
> had not heard a thing. No messenger brought the truth
> of how her husband made his stand outside the gates.
> She was weaving at her loom, deep in the high halls,
> working flowered braiding into a dark red folding robe.
> And she called her well-kempt women through the house
> to set a large three-legged cauldron over the fire
> so Hector could have his steaming hot bath
> when he came home from battle—poor woman,
> she never dreamed how far he was from bathing,
> struck down at Achilles' hands by blazing-eyed Athena.
>
> *Iliad* 22 514–524

It's another George-with-a-bullet-through-his-heart moment.

The Andromache-Hector love is domestic, tender: the love between Achilles and Patroclus passionate, extreme, filtered for the reader not so much through their companionship—bearing in mind that Achilles is absent from much of the poem—but largely through his superhuman sense of loss after Patroclus' death.

I am treading lightly here on dangerous territory: though the later

Greeks seemed to have no doubt in their minds that Achilles and Patroclus loved each other, and indeed were lovers, this is far from universally accepted today. I remember being at a press conference at the Cannes festival for the film *Troy*, at which the correspondent for the *Financial Times*, a classicist (God bless him) stood up and demanded of the filmmakers why there was no hint of homosexuality in the film's depiction of Achilles and Patroclus' relationship. The screenwriter and director practically thumped the table. "Show me the line! Show me the line in Homer where it says they are having a homosexual relationship!"

My own feeling is that Patroclus and Achilles love each other, deeply and completely. The poem doesn't make sense to me if they don't. The strength of feeling between Achilles and Patroclus is utterly clear. When Patroclus sees the devastation visited on the Greeks by the Trojans at the beginning of Book 16, Achilles (even though he is a particularly untender fellow) greets his friend with a wonderfully tender simile—why are you in tears, Patroclus, like a baby girl clinging onto her mother's skirts, begging to be picked up?

It's after Patroclus' death, though, that Achilles' love is unleashed in a terrible outpouring of grief and anger. He throws himself on to the ground and heaps filth and ashes over himself; his friend Antilochus, who brings him the news, grabs at his wrists so that Achilles won't slaughter him on the spot in his frenzy. His wrenching cry of grief is so powerful that his mother, deep in the ocean, hears him. The next morning he is still clutching Patroclus' body, weeping. His killing spree is a grotesque, appalling attempt not only to avenge himself, but to dull the pain of loss. In Book 23—after he has clotted the river Scamander with the blood of Trojans, and slaughtered Hector—Achilles goes down to the beach and lies down to try to get some rest. Patroclus' ghost appears, and begs his companion that they, when the time comes, should be buried together: surely a signal of their utter devotion. Achilles answers:

165

"I will obey you, your demands, Oh come closer!
Throw our arms around each other, just for a moment—take
some joy in the tears that numb the heart!"
In the same breath he stretched his loving arms
but could not seize him, no, the ghost slipped underground
like a wisp of smoke . . . with a high thin cry.

Iliad 23 114–118

GREEK HOMOSEXUALITY

Benjamin Jowett: . . . Nowhere was the ideal of morality, art
and social order realised more harmoniously than in Greece in
the age of the great philosophers.
John Ruskin: Buggery apart.
Jowett: Buggery apart.

Tom Stoppard: *The Invention of Love*

Greek homosexuality has long been an intellectual battle-
ground. In conventional Victorian thinking, the fact that
sexual relationships between Greek men were commonplace,
indeed encouraged and celebrated, was a hideous blot on an
otherwise deeply admirable society. And today, research into
ancient sexuality feeds directly into modern debates, in particular those about whether sexuality is intrinsic and unvary-
ing through time and in different societies (as "essentialists"
argue); or is contingent on particular cultural circumstance (as
"constructionists" contend).

What seems clear, at least, is the historical fact that in Athens (and, as with so many aspects of Greek society, there were
many local variants of custom and habit) youths were admiringly pursued by slightly older men, who had plenty of op-
portunities to gaze on the muscular young flesh of their loved
ones as it became hardened and defined through exercise in
the gymnasium. A young man might in time favor his older
admirer—with his company, conversation, and possibly with
sex. In Sparta, meanwhile (to take another example), military

discipline and education were fostered by relationships between older and younger officers. And in Thebes and Elis there were "armies of lovers"—contingents of champions, sacred bands composed entirely of *erastai* (lovers) and *eromenoi* (the beloved). There was love between women, too, clearly discernible in Sappho's poems, in which the narrator often alludes to her passionate desire for girls.

For some, the question has been whether "Greek homosexuality" can be thought of as homosexuality at all—at least as we understand it in the modern world. Its patterns can look rather alien, after all, with its older *erastai* in pursuit of its younger *eromenoi* (and hardly ever the other way around). And for modern gay politics, clearly this matters. Can Greek homosexuality be claimed as the antecedent of modern homosexuality at all? And what about the faintly troubling notion that the Greeks publicly celebrated the love of boys? Does this not have a whiff of pederasty about it?

An extremely important marker was put down in the study of ancient sexuality by Kenneth Dover's book *Greek Homosexuality* (1978). It was taken on board in its entirety by Michel Foucault, heavily influencing that writer's *History of Sexuality*, and so has exerted a huge influence on historians and sociologists ever since. Dover saw Greek homosexuality broadly in terms of a hierarchy of active and passive partners, the lover and the loved, the penetrator and the penetratee. To be penetrated, he argued, was to be humiliated. However, not all scholars have agreed with that picture. Notably, James Davidson, in his 2007 book *The Greeks and Greek Love*, sought to draw a more nuanced map of Greek homosexuality, with the focus less on the nitty-gritty of the sexual act and who did what to whom, and more on love, affection, and devotion. He broadened the picture to look at same-sex marriage ceremonies in Crete, for example, and reminded readers that there were long-term devoted relationships such as that between Pausanias and Agathon, vividly conjured up in Plato's *Symposium*. He also argued that the Athenians, for instance, would have been unlikely to have tolerated sexual relationships involving boys under eighteen.

I can't help feeling reminded by Patroclus' evanescence of the nature of our own relationship with the Greek world. We try to grasp it; it quivers and spins away from us, not to be pinned down or fully known. So much of Sappho's poetry is about love, but love as an absence, as a loss, as a state of longing, but never quite of achieving, the loved one—as in this fragment:

> Like the sweet apple reddening on the topmost branch,
> the topmost apple on the tip of the branch,
> and the pickers forgot it,
> well, no, they didn't forget, they just couldn't reach it.

That's the classicist-poet Stanley Lombardo's translation. Sappho is, we can guess, comparing a young girl to this delicious, but unobtainable fruit.

Lombardo's translations of Sappho's poems manage to convey beautifully the friable, in-pieces nature of her work, as we have them today. If you flick through a text of Sappho, you realize that they exist, for the most part, as tiny shards. In antiquity, Sappho was known as an extremely prolific and high-quality poet. In the great library in Alexandria, in the Hellenistic era, there were supposedly nine complete scrolls of poems by her. But nine volumes is very far from what we have today. There are one or two complete or very nearly complete poems, but much of what we have are lines, half lines, or even single words. These have been gathered painstakingly from delicate, damaged pieces of papyri, or found quoted in the work of other authors—in books on literary style, say, or as in-passing examples in ancient handbooks on grammar, etymology, or spelling. In the case of the poem invoking Aphrodite quoted on page 75, the text was found in the 1930s on an ancient rubbish tip, scribbled out on some broken pot. The excavators knew it was by Sappho because a shorter fragment of the same poem had long been in circulation.

Somehow these tiny scraps have a resonance and wonderment all their own. "I long and I yearn"; "you burn me"; "with what eyes"— each frail fragment sets off a chain reaction in the imagination; and, to me at least, a sense of loss, a sense of desire for completion that can never be fulfilled.

Here's another Lombardo translation of one of Sappho's most famous poems, which we have more or less in full because it was admiringly quoted by the Roman-era literary critic Longinus in his book *On the Sublime*:

Look at him, just like a god,
that man sitting across from you,
whoever he is,
                listening to your
                   close, sweet voice,
your irresistible laughter
                       And O yes,
it sets my heart racing—
                  one glance at you
and I can't get any words out,
                my voice cracks,
a thin flame runs under my skin,
my eyes go blind,
              my ears ring,
a cold sweat pours down my body,
I tremble all over,
              turn paler than grass.
Look at me
              just a shade from dead
But I must bear it, since a poor

The narrator sits watching her loved one conversing with a man— godlike perhaps in his beauty, or more likely in his good fortune.

Sappho wants the girl, she can't have her . . . she can see her but she's inaccessible, out of reach, like the apple on the topmost bough.

The most famous Greek text on desire, perhaps, is the *Symposium*, Plato's beautiful, moving, and often very funny dialogue on the philosophy of love. The scene is a dinner party in Athens, at the house of Agathon, a tragic playwright. Instead of drinking themselves silly, the guests, at the suggestion of the doctor Eryximachus, each decide to give a speech in praise of Eros. Eros makes even cowards strong, says Phaedrus; lovers make the best soldiers. Eros is in everything, says Eryximachus: it is a force governing the body and good health; it even governs musical harmony and rhythm. When he has recovered from the hiccups, Aristophanes, the comic playwright, proposes the wonderful idea that every human is but half a being, that we were once separated from our "other halves." If someone does have the good fortune to find their "other half," "it's impossible to describe the affection, warmth, and love they feel for each other; it's hardly an exaggeration to say that they don't want to spend even a moment apart." According to Agathon, on the other hand, Eros has only to touch you and you will become a poet. "He dispenses mildness and dismisses wildness; he is unsparing of goodwill and unsharing of ill-will. He is gracious and gentle; adored by the wise, admired by the gods, craved when absent, prized when present."

Finally comes Socrates' speech. Eros, he argues, is a desire for something lacking. For instance, if you were tall already, you wouldn't desire tallness. Eros is not-having; the force field, as it were, that exists between the lover and the object of his love. He starts to tell a story that he says he heard from one Diotima, a woman wise in many fields, but especially in love. *She* argued, said Socrates, that since Eros desired qualities such as attractiveness and goodness, he could not properly be called a god, since no god is anything less than completely good or attractive. Instead, Eros exists in between gods and men, as an intermediary. Diotima, according to Socrates, describes how a lover will at first focus on the attractive physical qualities of his loved one. This will lead him, eventually, to start to think about not just beauty in a particular instance, but beauty in general, beauty itself, the idea—or Form (see chapter 8)—of beauty. "He'll perceive it in itself and by itself, constant and eternal, and he'll see that every other beautiful object somehow partakes of it."

She continues. The right kind of Eros, she says,

". . . can help you ascend from the things of this world until you begin to catch sight of that beauty, and then you're almost within striking distance of the goal. The proper way to go about or be guided through the ways of love [eros] is to start with beautiful things in this world and always make the beauty I've been talking about the reason for your ascent. You start by loving one attractive body and step up to two; from there you move on to the beauty of people's activities, from there to the beauty of intellectual endeavours, and from there you ascend to that final intellectual endeavour, which is no more and no less than the study of that beauty, so that you finally recognise true beauty."

Symposium 211 b–c
Translation: Robin Waterfield

It's the most powerful and moving account of the intertwining of Eros and intellectual enlightenment: the idea that Eros is the force that can help us ascend from ignorance to knowledge; that love and knowledge are inextricably linked. And yet Love, Eros, is also a state of lack, of not-having. Eros will for ever be tinged with loss. Just as we shall never quite possess the loved one, we will never quite inhabit the realm of Forms.

For me, it is like our relationship with what we call "ancient

Greece." We forever attempt to possess it; but we never altogether shall, though the desire for it is a wonderful and enlightening and enriching state. Like Sappho's inaccessible lover, it will always be just out of reach. Like Patroclus' ghost, it will forever slip gently through our fingers.

TIMELINE

776 Olympic Games founded

c. 750 Greek alphabet

c. 700 Homeric epics written down?
  Hesiod composes *Works and Days* and *Theogony*

Second half seventh century Sappho

c. 620 Draco codifies laws in Athens

600 Thales of Miletus

594 Solon overturns Draco's law code
  Political reforms

557 Accession of Cyrus of Persia

c. 546 Cyrus defeats Croesus of Lydia

545–510 Pisistradid tyranny in Athens

530 Accession of Cambyses of Persia

521 Accession of Darius of Persia

508/7 Cleisthenes' reforms in Athens (emergence of democratic system)

499–494 Revolt by Greek cities in Ionia (western Turkey) against Persian rule

490 Persian Wars: battle of Marathon

486 Accession of Xerxes of Persia

480 Battles of Thermopylae and Salamis

479 Battle of Plataea

478 Athens founds Delian League

462 Ephialtes and Pericles introduce further democratic reform in Athens

458 Aeschylus *Oresteia*

454 Delian League treasury is moved from Delos to Athens

447 Work begins on Parthenon (completed 432)

?441 Sophocles *Antigone*

431 Peloponnesian War (to 404)
  Euripides *Medea*

c. 425 Herodotus completes *Histories*

423 Aristophanes *Clouds*

415 Athenian expedition to Sicily
  Euripides *Trojan Women*

411 Democracy overturned in Athens, regime of 400

410 Democracy restored in Athens

406 Euripides *Bacchae*

404 Athens' final defeat in the Peloponnesian War
   Rule of the Thirty Tyrants in Athens

403 Democracy restored in Athens

401 Sophocles *Oedipus of Colonus* (posthumous premiere)

400 Thucydides dies, his account of the Peloponnesian War unfinished

399 Death of Socrates

Early fourth century Plato's dialogues including *Apology, Phaedo, Symposium, Republic*

c. 385 Plato founds Academy

359 Accession of Philip II of Macedon

338 Battle of Chaeroneia
   Philip of Macedon becomes ruler of the Greek world

336 Accession of Alexander the Great

c. 335 Aristotle founds Lyceum

323 Alexander dies

322 Final defeat of Greek cities by Macedonians
   End of Athenian democracy
   Death of Aristotle

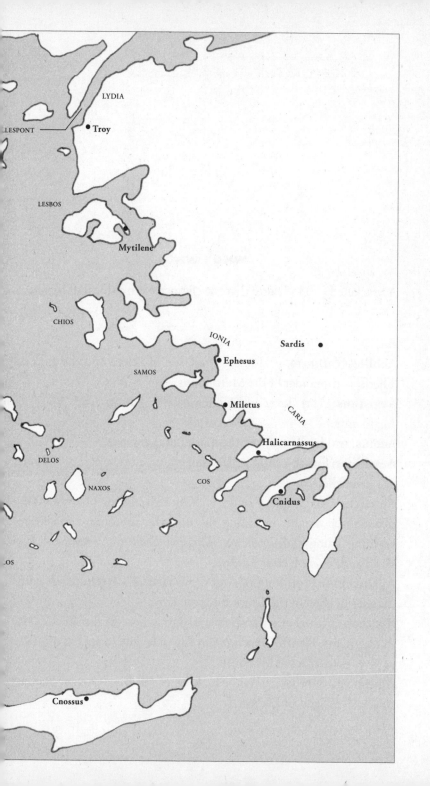

WHO'S WHO

A bracketed (m) indicates that the character is mythical or literary

A

Achilles: (m) hero of Homer's *Iliad*, son of Peleus and the goddess Thetis, commander of the Myrmidons.

Aegisthus: (m) lover of Clytemnestra, cousin and killer of Agamemnon.

Aeolus: (m) in the *Odyssey*, the master of the winds.

Aeschines: fourth-century Athenian orator, contemporary and rival of Demosthenes

Aeschylus: tragic playwright, c. 525–455, author of over ninety plays, seven extant, including the *Oresteia*, the only complete remaining trilogy (*Agamemnon, Libation Bearers, Eumenides*); *Persians*; and *Seven Against Thebes*.

Agamemnon: (m) king of Argos, husband of Clytemnestra, commander in chief of the Greek forces at Troy.

Agathon: fifth-century tragic playwright whose works survive only in fragments. Plato's *Symposium*, in which he gives a speech in praise of love, takes place at his house.

Agave: (m) mother of Pentheus, king of Thebes, sister of Semele, mother, by Zeus, of Dionysus.

Ajax, the greater: (m) son of Telemon, Greek commander in the *Iliad*.

Ajax, the lesser: (m) son of Oileus, Greek commander in the *Iliad*.

Alcinous: (m) in the *Odyssey*, king of the Phaeacians, husband of Arete, father of Nausicaa.

Alexander (1): "the Great." Macedonian king, 356–323, one of the most successful military commanders of all time, whose conquests included the Persian empire and Egypt and extended as far east as the Punjab.

Alexander (2): Macedonian king, 498–454.

Alcmena: (m) mother of Heracles.

Anaxagoras: fifth-century thinker and associate of Pericles.

Anaximander: sixth-century Milesian thinker, author of *On the Nature of Things*, posited a mechanical model for the movement of the heavenly bodies.

Anaximenes: sixth-century Milesian thinker, offered the idea of air as the basic material of the universe.

Andromache: (m) wife of Hector, mother of Astyanax.

Antigone: (m) daughter of Oedipus of Thebes and Jocasta; niece of Creon, fiancée of Haemon. Eponymous heroine of a play by Sophocles.

Antilochus: (m) in the *Iliad*, son of Nestor and friend of Achilles.

Aphrodite: (m) goddess.

Apollo: (m) god.

Archidamus: Spartan king (reigned c. 469–427) after whom the first phase of the Peloponnesian War is named.

Ares: (m) god.

Arete: (m) in the *Odyssey*, queen of the Phaeacians, husband of Alcinous, mother of Nausicaa.

Argeleonis: mother of the Spartan general Brasidas, who fought in the first phase of the Peloponnesian War. To her was attributed the command: "Come back with your shield—or on it."

Argos: (m) in the *Odyssey*, Odysseus' dog.

Arion: in Herodotus, a musician at the court of the seventh/sixth-century tyrant Periander of Corinth.

Aristagoras: deputy tyrant of Miletus, c. 505–496, said by Herodotus to have been the originator of the Ionian Revolt.

Aristogiton: with his lover Harmodius, assassin in 514 of Hipparchus, brother of Hippias, tyrant of Athens.

Aristotle: philosopher, scientist, literary critic, political theorist, tutor of Alexander the Great, 384–322.

Aristophanes: Athenian comic playwright, c. 445–386, eleven of whose plays survive, including *Clouds, Acharnians, Frogs*, and *Lysistrata*.

Aristodamus: one of the two Spartan survivors of the battle of Thermopylae (480).

Artemisia: queen of Halicarnassus (now Bodrum) in the early fifth century. In Herodotus, tactical adviser to Xerxes of Persia.

Asclepius: (m) god of healing, who reputedly learnt his skills from Chiron the centaur.

Aspasia: lover of Pericles.

Astyages: late seventh-century king of the Medes, grandfather of Cyrus of Persia.

Astyanax: (m) son of Andromache and Hector of Troy.

Athena: (m) goddess.

Atossa: wife of Darius of Persia, daughter of Cyrus the Great.

Atropos: (m) one of the Fates.

B

Biton: an Argive athlete said by Solon (in Herodotus) to have been, with his brother Cleobis, the second-happiest man in the world.

Brasidas: Spartan military leader in the first phase of the Peloponnesian War.

Briseis: (m) in the *Iliad*, Trojan captive of Achilles.

C

Calypso: (m) in the *Odyssey*, nymph.

Cambyses: king of Persia (succeeded in 530), son of Cyrus.

Candaules: eighth-century king of Lydia.

Cassandra: (m) Trojan princess, daughter of Priam and Hecuba.

Castor: (m) twin of Polydeuces, brother of Clytemnestra and Helen.

Cephalus: wealthy resident of Athens at whose house Plato's *Republic* is set.

Cerberus: (m) three-headed dog who guards the entrance to the Underworld.

Chaerephon: friend of Socrates, who consulted the Delphic oracle to discover whether there was anyone wiser than he.

Charybdis: (m) monster, in the *Odyssey*, in the form of a giant whirlpool.

Chiron: (m) ferryman who conveys souls over the River Styx to the Underworld.

Circe: (m) in the *Odyssey*, witch.

Cleisthenes: Athenian whose wide-ranging reforms in 508/7 are credited with creating democracy.

Cleobis: an Argive athlete said by Solon (in Herodotus) to have been, with his brother Biton, the second-happiest man in the world.

Cleomenes: king of Sparta c. 520–490, father of Gorgo, wife of King Leonidas.

Clotho: (m) one of the Fates.

Clytemnestra: (m) wife of Agamemnon, sister of Helen.

Creon: (m) king of Thebes after the exile of his brother-in-law Oedipus. Uncle of Antigone.

Critias: Plato's uncle; one of the Thirty Tyrants who took over Athens in 404.

Crito: friend of Socrates, present at his execution.

Croesus: legendarily wealthy king of Lydia defeated by the growing Persian empire in 545.

Cronus: (m) Titan god, husband and brother of Rhea, father of Zeus, Hera, Poseidon, Hades, Hestia, and Demeter.

Cylon: seventh-century Athenian who attempted to take over as tyrant.

Cynisca: Spartan woman who trained a team of horses, victorious in the Olympic Games of 396 and 392.

Cyrus: "the Great," founder of the Persian empire, ruled 557–530.

D

Danaë: (m) mother, by Zeus, of the hero Perseus.

Darius: nobleman who, after a bloody struggle, ruled Persia 522–486.

Demaratus: Spartan king who defected to the Persians; in Herodotus acts as adviser to Xerxes.

Demeter: (m) goddess.

Democedes: in Herodotus, doctor employed by Polycrates, sixth-century tyrant of Samos.

Democritus: fifth century thinker, atomist.

Demodocus: (m) in the *Odyssey*, bard at the court of Alcinous and Arete.

Dicaeopolis: (m) hero of Aristophanes' play *Acharnians*.

Diomedes: (m) in the *Iliad*, Greek commander, son of Tydeus.

Dione: (m) goddess, in the *Iliad*, the mother of Aphrodite.

Dionysus: (m) god.

Diotima: (possibly m) in Plato's *Symposium*, priestess of Mantinea, from whom Socrates claims to have learned his theory of love.

Dolon: (m) in the *Iliad*, Trojan spy captured and killed by Odysseus and Diomedes.

Draco: the Athenian who, by tradition, set down the first Athenian law code in 621/0.

E

Electra: (m) daughter of Agamemnon and Clytemnestra, sister of Orestes. Subject of plays by Sophocles and Euripides.

Empedocles: fifth-century thinker who propounded the notions of the elements earth, air, fire, and water.

Ephialtes: Malian who betrayed the Greeks at Thermopylae, indicating a little-known mountain route to the Spartans' rear to the Persians.

Eros: (m) god.

Eryximachus: fifth-century Athenian doctor; character in Plato's *Symposium*.

Eteocles: (m) prince of Thebes, son of Oedipus, brother of Polynices and Antigone.

Eudoxus: fourth-century mathematician and astronomer who proposed a theory to explain the "retrogression" of planets.

Eumaeus: (m) in the *Odyssey*, swineherd of Ithaca.

Eumenides: (m) "the kindly ones" into which the vengeance-seeking Furies are transformed in Aeschylus' *Oresteia*.

Euripides: tragic playwright, 480s–407. Author of ninety plays, twenty extant, including *Bacchae, Trojan Women, Medea, Hippolytus, Iphigenia at Aulis, Iphigenia at Tauris, Heracles, Ion*.

Eurybiades: Spartan; commander of the Greek fleet at Artemisium and Salamis.

Eurycleia: (m) in the *Odyssey*, Odysseus' nurse.

Eurypylus: (m) in the *Iliad*, friend of Patroclus.

Eurystheus: (m) king of Argos who set Heracles' labours.

G

Ganymede: (m) beautiful Trojan prince abducted by Zeus to become the gods' cupbearer.

Glauce: (m) princess who became Jason's second wife after he abandoned Medea.

Glaucon: brother of Plato, friend of Socrates. One of the latter's interlocutors in the *Republic*.

Glaucus: (m) a sea god, alluded to in Plato's *Republic*.

Gorgo: fifth-century Spartan queen, wife of Leonidas.

Gorgons: (m) female monsters, among whom was Medusa, who could turn a mortal to stone with her glance.

Gorgythion: (m) in the *Iliad*, a Trojan killed by Teucer, strikingly compared to a poppy at 8 344.

Gyges: late eighth/early seventh-century king of Lydia, deposer of Candaules.

H

Hades: (m) god.

Haemon: (m) prince of Thebes, son of Creon, fiancé of Antigone.

Harmodius: with his lover Aristogiton, assassin in 514 of Hipparchus, brother of Hippias, tyrant of Athens.

Hebe: (m) goddess.

Hector: (m) Trojan prince and champion, son of Priam and Hecuba, husband of Andromache, father of Astyanax.

Hecuba: (m) Trojan queen, wife of Priam, mother of Hector.

Helen: (m) daughter of Zeus and Leda, wife of Menelaus of Sparta. Her abduction by Paris caused the Trojan war.

Helios: (m) sun god.

Hephaestus: (m) god.

Hera: (m) goddess.

Heraclitus: early-fifth-century thinker who held that the universe was in a state of constant flux.

Heracles: (m) hero, son of Zeus and Alcmena, famed for, amongst other things, his twelve labors.

Hermes: (m) god.

Hermias: fourth-century tyrant of Atarneus and patron of Aristotle.

Herodotus: Halicarnassus-born author of *The Histories*, an account of the Persian Wars, later organized into nine books. 480–425.

Hestia: (m) goddess.

Hipparchus: son of Pisistratus, brother of Hippias, tyrants of Athens. Assassinated by the lovers Harmodius and Aristogiton in 514.

Hippias: son of Pisistratus, brother of Hipparchus, tyrant of Athens 527–510.

Hippocrates: doctor in the second half of the fifth century. Born in Cos. The body of medical writings known as the Hippocratic Corpus is traditionally attributed to him.

Homer: poet, traditionally said to have been born on Chios, possibly working at the end of the eighth century, to whom the *Iliad* and the *Odyssey* have traditionally been attributed.

Hyacinthus: (m) mortal, accidentally killed by his lover, the god Apollo, with a blow from a discus.

Hydra: (m) hundred-headed monster.

I

Iphigenia: (m) daughter of Agamemnon and Clytemnestra, sacrificed by her father at Aulis to secure the Greek fleet a fair wind to Troy. Subject of two plays by Euripides.

Iris: (m) goddess.

J

Jason: (m) hero, son of Aeson, leader of the Argonauts in their quest to retrieve the Golden Fleece from Colchis on the Black Sea.

Jocasta: (m) wife and mother of Oedipus, mother of Antigone, Ismene, Eteocles, and Polynices.

L

Lachesis: (m) one of the Fates.

Laertes: (m) in the *Odyssey*, father of Odysseus.

Laestrygonians: (m) in the *Odyssey*, a race of cannibals who consume Odysseus' entire fleet with the exception of his own ship.

Laius: (m) husband of Jocasta, father of Oedipus.

Leda: (m) mother of Helen of Troy and Clytemnestra

Leucippus: fifth-century thinker, atomist.

Leonidas: King of Sparta, who led the 300 against the Persians at Thermopylae in 480. Husband of Gorgo.

Lycaon: (m) a son of Priam, killed by Achilles in *Iliad* Book 20.

Lycurgus: (m?) according to the Spartans, the originator of their constitution.

Lysias: son of Cephalus (qv); character in Plato's *Republic*.

M

Machaon: (m) in the *Iliad*, Greek doctor, brother of Polidarius, son of Asclepius.

Mardonius: cousin of Xerxes of Persia, commander of the Persian troops in 479 at Plataea, where he was killed.

Medea: (m) daughter of Aeëtes, king of Colchis, whence she helped Jason secure the Golden Fleece. Later killed Jason and their children. Subject of a play by Euripides.

Medusa: (m) one of the Gorgons (qv).

Menelaus: (m) king of Sparta, brother of Agamemnon, husband of Helen.

Merope: (m) queen of Corinth, wife of Polybus, at whose court Oedipus was brought up.

N

Nausicaa: (m) in the *Odyssey*, daughter of King Alcinous and Queen Arete of the Phaeacians.

Nereus: (m) god; the "old man of the sea."

Nestor: (m) king of Pylos, father of Antilochus.

O

Odysseus: (m) son of Laertes, husband of Penelope, king of Ithaca. Commander of Ithacan troops in the *Iliad*; hero of the *Odyssey*.

Oedipus: (m) son of Laius and Jocasta; also husband of Jocasta. Hero of two extant plays by Sophocles.

Omphale: (m) queen of Lydia for whom Heracles was obliged to work, in drag.

P

Pandarus: (m) in the *Iliad*, the Trojan archer who breaks the truce in Book 4.

Pandora: (m) in Hesiod, the first woman. Let all the evils of the world out of her jar; only hope remained under the lip.

Pantites: Spartan survivor of the battle of Thermopylae.

Paris: (m) son of Priam and Hecuba, prince of Troy. His abduction of Helen, wife of Menelaus, led to the Trojan war.

Parmenides: early-fifth-century thinker. Worked in southern Italy.

Patroclus: (m) son of Menoetius. In the *Iliad*, companion of Achilles, killed by Hector.

Penelope: (m) wife of Odysseus.

Pentheus: (m) king of Thebes, son of Agave, nephew of Semele, cousin of the god Dionysus. Principal character in Euripides' *Bacchae*.

Pericles: c. 495–429. Athenian general, politician, statesman. Thucydides, in his *History of the Peloponnesian War*, puts into his mouth the famous funeral oration mourning the Athenian dead.

Persephone: (m) goddess.

Perseus: (m) son of Danaë and Zeus, slayer of the Gorgon Medusa.

Phaedymia: daughter of the Persian noble Otanes, who identified Cambyses of Persia's successor, Smerdis, as an impostor.

Phaedo: friend of Socrates; gives his name to the Platonic dialogue recounting Socrates' death.

Phaedrus: Athenian, member of Socrates' circle, born c. 450, who gave his name to a famous Platonic dialogue.

Pherecydes: reputedly the first writer, in the mid-sixth century, of Greek prose.

Philip of Macedon: 382–336. King and successful military commander who, at the battle of Chaeronea in 338, became the master of the Greek world.

Philippides: Athenian messenger during the Persian Wars whose twenty-six-mile run in 490 between the battlefield of Marathon and Athens gave us the race.

Phoenix: (m) in the *Iliad*, tutor and comrade of Achilles.

Phryne: famous Athenian courtesan.

Pindar: poet, c. 522–443, composer of hymns, paeans, victory odes.

Pisistratus: tyrant of Athens, c. 546–527. Father of Hippias and Hipparchus.

Plato: philosopher, c. 429–347, author of numerous works mostly in dialogue form, including *Apology, Phaedo, Republic, Symposium, Phaedrus*.

Plutarch: first- to second-century AD Greek biographer.

Podalirius: (m) doctor in the *Iliad*, brother of Machaon, son of Asclepius.

Polemarchus: son of Cephalus (qv); character in Plato's *Republic*.

Polybus: (m) a king of Corinth, who brought up Oedipus.

Polycrates: tyrant of Samos, 535–522.

Polydeuces: (m) twin of Castor, brother of Clytemnestra and Helen.

Polynices: (m) prince of Thebes, son of Oedipus, brother of Antigone and Eteocles.

Polyphemus: (m) in the *Odyssey*, Cyclops. Son of Poseidon.

Poseidon: (m) god.

Praxiteles: celebrated Athenian sculptor, active c. 375–330.

Priam: (m) king of Troy, husband of Hecuba, father of Hector and Cassandra.

Prometheus: (m) Titan who stole fire from the gods.

Protagoras: c. 490–420. Most famous of the sophists, credited with developing relativism and famous for the doctrine "man is the measure of all things."

Pythagoras: sixth-century Samian religious leader and mathematician.

Pythia, the: priestess of Apollo at Delphi, conduit of the god's prophecies.

R

Rhea: (m) Titan goddess, sister and wife of Cronus, mother of Zeus, Hera, Poseidon, Hades, Hestia, and Demeter.

S

Sappho: lyric poet born on Lesbos in the second half of the seventh century; hailed as the "tenth Muse."

Sarpedon: (m) in the *Iliad*, son of Zeus and commander of the Lycians, allies of Troy.

Scamander: in the *Iliad*, river near Troy that fights Achilles.

Scylla: (m) six-headed, mariner-munching female monster inhabiting a cave opposite Charybdis (qv).

Semele: (m) daughter of Cadmus of Thebes; mother, by Zeus, of the god Dionysus.

Socrates: Athenian philosopher, 469–399. Left no writings; immortalized in the works of Plato.

Solon: Athenian politician, reformer, and poet active in the sixth century.

Sophocles: Athenian author of 123 plays, seven extant, including *Antigone, Oedipus the King, Oedipus at Colonus*, and *Philoctetes*. c. 495–406.

Strepsiades: (m) hero of Aristophanes' play *Clouds*.

T

Telemachus: (m) in the *Odyssey*, son of Odysseus and Penelope.

Tellus: an Athenian said by Solon (in Herodotus) to have been the happiest of all men.

Tethys: (m) sea goddess inhabiting ocean depths.

Thales: sixth-century scholar of Miletus, credited with the earliest Greek forays into scientific thinking.

Themistocles: c. 524–459. Athenian politician and military commander said by Herodotus to have been responsible for the creation of Athens' navy. Ostracized and later condemned to death *in absentia* by the Athenians.

Thersites: (m) in the *Iliad*, rank-and-file soldier who rails against the kings in Book 2 and is put down by Odysseus.

Thetis: (m) goddess.

Thrasymachus: sophist. Character in Plato's *Republic*.

Thucydides: late 450s–c. 400. Athenian general and author of *History of the Peloponnesian War*, later organized into eight books, incomplete at his death. Exiled from Athens for failing to save Amphipolis from the Spartan general Brasidas in 424.

Tiresias: (m) blind seer, at one time a woman, whose ghost is consulted by Odysseus in the *Odyssey* and who appears in plays about Thebes, such as *Oedipus the King* and *Bacchae*.

Titans: (m) the generation of gods preceding the Olympians, and including Cronus and Rhea.

X

Xanthippe: wife of Socrates.

Xenophanes: sixth-century poet and natural philosopher born in Colophon in Ionia. Famously criticized Homer and Hesiod for portraying gods as like flawed mortals.

Xenophon: Athenian writer, c. 430–355, of historical and biographical works.

Xerxes: king of Persia 486–465, son of Darius and Atossa.

Z

Zeno: early fifth-century thinker famous for formulating "Zeno's paradoxes."

Zephyrus: (m) the West Wind.

Zeus: (m) god.

Zopyrus: in Herodotus, the general responsible for the Persian breakthrough in the siege of Babylon.

KNOW YOUR GREEK GODS

The Twelve Olympians

Zeus: king of the gods, son of Rhea and Cronus, whom he deposed. Father, cloud-gatherer. Protector of justice, and of host-guest relationships. Often seen with a thunderbolt.

Hera: daughter of Cronus and Rhea, wife of Zeus. Queenly, noble, "ox-eyed," protector of marriage. Especially in later art, sometimes accompanied by peacocks.

Poseidon: brother of Zeus. Earth-shaker, god of the sea and of horses. Often seen with a trident.

Athena: born from the head of Zeus. Battle-loving, hero-helping, intelligent, cunning, skilled. Often seen wearing a helmet, carrying a spear and accompanied by an owl.

Ares: son of Zeus and Hera. God of war, destructive, insatiable, terrifying. Seen in full armor.

Artemis: daughter of Zeus and Leto. Virgin, hunter. In charge of female rites of passage such as childbirth. Brings sudden death to women. Often seen with bow and arrows, and in a short tunic.

Apollo: twin brother of Artemis. God of healing, prophecy, music, poetry. Plague-sender and plague-averter. Often seen with bow and arrows or a lyre.

Aphrodite: either born from blood from the severed genitals of Ocean as they were flung into the sea by Cronus, or daughter of Zeus and Dione. Seductively charming, sexy, adulterous. Goddess of love. Often seen with Eros, her young, mischievous companion.

Demeter: goddess of harvest, corn, fruitfulness, agriculture, civilization. Often seen with ears of corn.

Hephaestus: fatherless son of Hera. God of fire, a great craftsman. Cuckolded husband of Aphrodite. Often seen at his forge.

Dionysus: son of Zeus and Semele—"twice born" (because snatched from the womb of his dying mother and later born from his father's thigh). God of wine, intoxication, ecstasy. Contradictory—both terrible and sweet. Often seen drunk, with vines and an entourage of satyrs.

Hermes: son of Zeus and Maia. Messenger of Zeus, guide of travelers, ingenious, inventive. Protector of herds and flocks, bringer of good fortune and fertility. Often seen in winged sandals, or with a traveling hat and cloak.

AND ALSO . . .

Hades: son of Cronus and Rhea. If Zeus presides over the heavens, and Poseidon over the earth, Hades rules the third realm, the Underworld. Fearful, sinister, death personified.

Persephone: daughter of Demeter and wife, after he abducted her, of Hades. Spends four months of the year in the Underworld, bringing winter, and the remaining eight with her mother, bringing summer.

Hestia: daughter of Cronus and Rhea. Goddess of the hearth.

Hebe: daughter of Hera and Zeus. Goddess of youthfulness, sometime cupbearer of the gods.

Iris: rainbow goddess, messenger of the gods. "Storm-footed."

Eros: the oldest of the gods; or sometimes seen as the child, or youthful companion, of Aphrodite. God of desire.

The three Fates, who spin out men's destinies, are called Clotho (Spinner); **Lachesis** (Allotter); and **Atropos** (Inexorable).

The three Graces, who bring charm and beauty, are **Aglaea** (Radiance); **Euphrosyne** (Joy); and **Thalia** (Flowering).

The Muses, who bring creative inspiration, are:
Calliope (epic poetry)
Clio (history)
Euterpe (flute playing)
Terpsichore (dance)
Erato (lyric poetry)
Melpomene (tragedy)
Thalia (comedy)
Polyhymnia (hymns and pantomime)
Urania (astronomy)

KNOW THE GREEK IN YOUR ENGLISH

Spartan

As in, "Tarquin, I know the minimalist look is right up your street, but don't you think the room looks a little Spartan with the actual floorboards removed?"

Simple, severe, lacking in comfort: that does in fact pretty much sum up what we know about the life of the Spartans. Despite its position as a Greek military superpower, the place had none of the kind of impressive architecture that would have overwhelmed the eye of a late-fifth-century visitor to Athens. Famously, Sparta also lacked walls or fortifications (this was actually a show-off thing; it demonstrated that the inhabitants were such butch soldiers they didn't need any nancy-boy walls to keep them safe from aggressors). But being "Spartan" also meant adhering to an unbendable system of iron discipline, with boys taken out of their families for military training at the age of seven, and, uniquely for ancient Greece, girls also given an education and athletic training—the better, presumably, to give birth to warrior sons. This was the background that produced the toughies who, though vastly outnumbered, held off the Persians in 480 at the battle of Thermopylae, until, on the third day of the battle, all 300 (except the two who happened to be away from the scene at the time) were slaughtered. Dedication, bravery, and sheer suicidal bloodymindedness are thus also Spartan virtues.

Laconic

As in, "Darling, I know being a teenage boy is all about communicating in grunts, but if you could descend from your laconic monosyllables occasionally I'd be terribly grateful."

Laconia was the region of the southeast Peloponnese that Sparta controlled as her home territory; and our word "laconic" refers to another Spartan quality: a severe, economic, and sometimes dryly witty way with words. Not for the Spartans the flowing rills of rhetoric that the Athenians favored (and of course that so suited the speechifying politics of democracy). Spartans were short and to the point. There is a funny story (well, I find it funny) in Herodotus' *Histories*, Book 3, that illustrates this. Some islanders of Samos, who had been expelled by the tyrant Polycrates, went to Sparta to seek help. They made a long impassioned, eloquent speech outlining their cause. But the Spartans replied that they had forgotten the first part of the speech, and didn't understand the second part. So the Samians went off and put their heads together about how they could rephrase it in a suitably laconic manner, and they came back with the (admittedly rather cryptic): "This bag needs grain." The Spartans' reply this time was that the word "bag" was redundant . . .

Plutarch (or someone like him—the attribution is a bit shaky), writing some 500 years after Herodotus, actually collected a number of Spartan sayings—mostly spurious, no doubt, but very good lines anyway. They include the very laconic *molon labe* (it does sound better in Greek), which is what King Leonidas is supposed to have said at Thermopylae when Xerxes demanded the Spartans surrender their weapons. It means "Come and get them." Like many of these Plutarchian Spartan sayings, it was filched by the makers of the film *300* (see chapter 5). "Spartans, lay down your arms!" comes the cry. "Persians, come and get them!" replies Leonidas. The apothegm is today the motto of the Greek First Army Corps.

Sybaritic

As in, "Silk sheets and a jacuzzi. Some might say it was sybaritic. I'd call it a tart's boudoir."

Sybaris, now Sibari, was a Greek colony in southern Italy founded in about 720, and through its agricultural resources and trading connections with the Etruscans, it became a byword in antiquity for its luxury and decadence, its inhabitants famous for their gorgeous *haute couture* outfits. The good times didn't go on for ever: in about 510 the town was attacked and razed by Croton, another south-Italian Greek settlement.

Aegis

As in, "Don't worry, Henry, the animal care comes under the aegis of the National Donkey Protection League, which I am sure has impeccable standards."

Frankly, the aegis—a symbol of divine power—has always struck me as one of the weirdest things about the Greek gods. I can do no better than quote the estimable *Oxford Classical Dictionary*, which describes it as an "all-round bib with scales, fringed with snakes' heads and normally decorated with the *gorgoneion*." (*Gorgoneion* being classicist-speak for the head of the Gorgon Medusa.) The aegis, the entry helpfully adds, may sometimes be tasseled. Zeus sometimes wore it, as did Hephaestus, but it was most often sported by Athena, who was given Medusa's head by the hero Perseus after he decapitated her. Now why Athena would want to accessorize her normally stylish look with a bib—tasseled or otherwise—is beyond me. I have also heard the aegis described as looking like a kind of sporran.

Thespian

As in, "Brenda has marvelous talents as a thespian, you know. You should see her Lady Bracknell."

Thespis was the man who, according to Aristotle, "invented" Greek drama, adding a prologue and speech to what had previously been a choral performance. A date for this is hard to establish; perhaps it was the third quarter of the sixth century. Not to be confused with the Thespians who were the inhabitants of Thespiae, one of the few towns to send troops to Thermopylae to fight alongside the Spartans in 480.

Stygian

As in, "Hector dear, could you possibly put on another light? I can't see to read in this Stygian gloom."

Stygian is the adjective from Styx, the river that souls of the dead must cross to pass into the Underworld, and as miserable a place as one could imagine. The Styx was plied by Charon, and he only ever took two living mortals across—Orpheus, because the ferryman was bewitched by the beauty of his singing; and Heracles, out of sheer terror. The dead were supposed to be buried with an obol (a small coin) to pay the ferryman's fare.

Herculean

As in, "Cleaning the bathroom and kitchen floors, Muriel, seems to me to be a labor of Herculean proportions."

Hercules is the Romanized name of Heracles, the greatest of all heroes, and one of the few mortals to attain the status of a god. The labors, set him by Eurystheus, king of Argos, were twelve in number. If you can rattle these off you'll be doing well . . . He had to kill the Nemean lion and the Lernaean Hydra, capture the Erymanthian boar and the hind of Ceryneia, and kill the Stymphalian birds. He had to clean out the stables of Augeus, capture the Cretan bull, round up the horses of the Thracian Diomedes, steal the belt of the Amazon queen Hippolyta, herd the cattle of Geryon, fetch the apples of the Hesperides, and capture Cerberus.

Heracles had something of a problem with madness and mass murder: the labors were done to expiate the killing of his wife Megara and their children, which he committed in a bout of insanity visited on him by the goddess Hera. Another story has him killing the father and brothers of his girlfriend Iole. To purify himself from the pollution of that crime, he worked for the queen of Lydia, Omphale, for three years. The twist was that he had to do this servitude as a woman—doing spinning and weaving, in drag, a scene vividly depicted on a Roman wellhead in the Townley Collection of Roman antiquities in the basement of the British Museum.

Tantalizing

As in, "I've just caught a tantalizing glimpse of Frank's homemade apricot ice cream and I can't wait to taste it."

From Tantalus, one of the very first generations of mortals. Invited by the gods to dine on Mount Olympus, he decided to kill, cook, and serve up his son Pelops to see whether his hosts would detect the forbidden food (as you do). Demeter, distracted by her grief for her daughter Persephone, lately abducted by Hades, was the only immortal who tucked in, polishing off a shoulder. The gods reconstructed Pelops and brought him back to life—with a prosthetic shoulder made from ivory. Tantalus' eternal punishment in the Underworld was to stand in a pool that drained away when he tried to drink from it; and beneath branches groaning with fruit that drew away when he reached for them.

A tantalus is also a lockable stand for a set of decanters. You can see the booze, but you can't get at it without the key . . .

Sisyphean

As in, "The sodding lawn needs mowing every single week. It's a Sisyphean task."

Sisyphus was another of the earliest generations of mortals who tried to outwit the gods. According to some versions, he tied Death up so that no one (least of all he himself) could die, until the gods sent Ares to free him. Having done so, Ares sent Death straight back to Sisyphus. But Sisyphus had primed his wife not to give him funerary rites, so when he did arrive in the Underworld, he persuaded Hades to let him nip back up to complain. When he got there, of course, he stayed put, and lived a hearty life, dying in the end of old age. But his eternal punishment in the Underworld was to roll a huge boulder up a hill. Whenever he got it up to the top, it would roll straight back down and Sisyphus would have to start again.

Colossal

As in, "I'm heading for a colossal overdraft. Drinks on you, I'm afraid."

From the Colossus of Rhodes, one of the seven ancient wonders of the world. In 305, Rhodes was attacked by the Macedonian Demetrius Poliorcetes and successfully saw off a yearlong siege. Demetrius abandoned his siege equipment on the island, and the grateful Rhodians used the proceeds from the sale of all that to erect a thirty-three-meter statue to their patron, Helios the sun god, which they commissioned from the famous sculptor Chares of Lindos. Often depicted in later art as straddling the harbor entrance, it is much more likely to have been placed on a nearby promontory. However, it stood for only fifty-six years; an earthquake in about 226 undermined the statue at the knee. Even in ruins it still excited visitors, such as the Roman writer Pliny, who noted that its thumb was too big for most men to be able to clasp in their arms, and that its very fingers were bigger than most ordinary statues.

In the seventh century AD, Rhodes was conquered by Arabs who sold the statue as scrap metal. The other wonders of the world were the great pyramid of Giza, the lighthouse of Alexandria, the hanging gardens of Babylon, the walls of Babylon, the temple of Artemis at Ephesus, the mausoleum of Mausolus at Halicarnassus, and the statue of Zeus at Olympia. The Statue of Liberty is inspired by the Colossus of Rhodes.

Oedipus complex

As in, "Put that ax down, Benjy. If you want to work through your Oedipus complex, then why don't you run along and find mummy."

Surely this is Freud's most famous idea: the notion that on some deep, hidden or metaphorical level boys wish to kill their fathers and sleep with their mothers. The complex is named after Sophocles' play *Oedipus the King*, in which the hero does just that—though, at least on a straightforward reading of the drama, unwittingly through a series of terrible chances, rather than because he is acting on some primal urge. For Freud, though, Oedipus' "destiny moves us only because it might have been ours—because the oracle laid the same curse upon us before our birth as upon him. It is the fate of all of us, perhaps, to direct our first sexual impulse towards our mother and our first hatred and our first murderous wish against our father. Our dreams convince us that this is so." The female version of the complex is known as the Electra complex, after the daughter of Clytemnestra and Agamemnon. She appears in plays by Aeschylus, Sophocles, and Euripides condoning her brother Orestes' vengeful murder of their mother—in Euripides' version, actually grabbing the hesitant arm of her brother and guiding the sword.

Draconian

As in, "Please, Miss, don't you think punishing smoking with a public flogging is a bit draconian?"

Draco was the Athenian who, by tradition, set down the first Athenian law code in 621/0, the first time the city's laws had been put in writing and displayed in public. Evidence is thin as to what, in fact, these laws comprised: but according to tradition, it was the death penalty for pretty much everything, whether the offense was large or small. One Athenian in the fourth century quipped that Draco wrote his laws in blood rather than ink. "Draconian" is always a negative word in English, but if you turn it the other way round, of course, you could argue that setting forth a state's laws in public for the first time was, in its way, a reforming measure . . . though Draco's code was itself reformed soon enough, in 594/3, by Solon, who repealed everything except the law on homicide. The boy's name Draco, for understandable reasons, has failed to take off: though it was famously pulled into service by J. K. Rowling for one of her most memorable baddies, the sinister Draco Malfoy. This is not surprising, given that J. K. studied Classics and French at Exeter University, and is rumored to have based Dumbledore on the splendidly bearded Peter Wiseman, Exeter's classics professor emeritus.

Procrustean

As in, "Don't you think it's rather Procrustean to decide that every single real estate broker is the devil's spawn?"

Bit of a show-off word, this, meaning something like "ruthlessly enforcing conformity without regard for individual differences." The word derives from Procrustes, a mythological brigand who haunted the road between Eleusis and Athens. He would abduct his victims and force them down on a bed. If they were too short, he would stretch them out until they fit it; if too tall, he would trim them down a bit. Charming, no?

Ostracize

As in, "I should think you'll be completely ostracized from the golf club, Derek, if you go anywhere near it in those trousers."

Ostracism was a method by which, through the Athenian democratic reforms introduced by Cleisthenes in 508/7, a citizen could be exiled for ten years after a majority vote in the Assembly. The name of the chosen man was written on a shard of pottery, in Greek an *ostrakon*. Nearly 200 *ostraka* have been found in an Athenian well, with the name Themistocles written on them in a very few hands—presumably he was at the receiving end of a carefully orchestrated campaign.

Odeon

As in "What's on at the Odeon? I quite fancy catching *300* again there, nothing I like better than a pumped-up Spartan wearing leather knickers."

The notable cinema chain is named, ultimately, for one of the great buildings on the slopes of the Acropolis, the *odeion*, or music hall (and in fact, there were *odeia* in other Greek cities, too). The Athenian *odeion* was a square hall with pillars supposedly made from the masts of Persian ships taken at the battle of Salamis in the Persian Wars. Men and boys' choral competitions, part of the festival called the City Dionysia, were held there, as well as previews of the main tragic plays. Popcorn was not served.

Sphinx

As in, "Nancy, don't be so Sphinx-like, just spit it out, I can't bear it when you talk in riddles."

The Sphinx was usually a creature with a lion's body and a human, often female, head. The people of Thebes were terrorized by the Sphinx, until Oedipus came along and solved its riddle: what has four legs, three legs, and two legs? Answer: man—as a crawling child, an old man with a stick, and an adult. Ingres' fabulous painting of Oedipus and the Sphinx is in the Louvre.

Hoi polloi

As in, "Ivy says she can't bear to go shopping on a Saturday. The town center is just too full of hoi polloi, apparently."

Hoi polloi is Greek for "the many," meaning the ordinary people. Used with more than a soupçon of snobbery in English. To say "the hoi polloi," incidentally, is strictly speaking a gaffe, since it means "the the many," as *hoi* is the definite article.

Halcyon days

As in, "I look back on the halcyon days of our summer vacation with an almost tearful nostalgia."

The halycon was the kingfisher. According to Aristotle, "This bird breeds at the time of the winter solstice. Hence when calm weather occurs at this period, the name 'halcyon days' is given to the seven days preceding and seven days following the solstice." Charming, but even Aristotle didn't believe it.

Sword of Damocles

As in, "It's all very well being given this great promotion, but I constantly feel the sword of Damocles dangling over me."

Damocles was a flattering courtier in the court of Dionysius II, a tyrant of Syracuse in the fourth century. Dionysius suggested that they swap places for the day. Damocles was having great fun being waited on hand and foot, surrounded by gorgeous, sexy young men, being fed peeled grapes, etc., until he looked up and noticed a sharp sword dangling by a thread above his head—by way of an illustration of the terror and anxiety that power brings.

Gordian knot

As in, "Fred says he's fed up with debating the whys and the wherefores so he's just going to cut through the Gordian knot and start barking orders at people."

Phrygria, part of modern Turkey, was once without a king. An oracle said that the next person to drive an ox cart past would become their ruler. Ahmidas was that man, and he dedicated an ox cart in gratitude, tying it by a complicated knot to a post. A further oracle said that the person who could untie the knot would become ruler of all Asia. Passing through the city of Gordium in 333, Alexander the Great tried to untie the knot. Failing, he simply got out his sword and slashed through it.

Titanic

As in, "I've got a nasty feeling my bum doesn't just look big in this, it looks titanic."

The Titans were the generation of gods immediately preceding the Olympians, including Zeus' parents Cronos and Rhea. The war between the two generations, won by Zeus and his brothers Hades and Poseidon, was the original battle of the Titans. The defeated Titans were locked deep within the very nethermost regions of Tartarus. When you think about it, not necessarily the most propitious name for a ship.

Achilles' heel

As in, "My Achilles' heel is that I'm rubbish at math and haven't the remotest sense of direction."

Achilles, the greatest warrior of the Trojan War, had been dipped into the waters of the river Styx by his goddess mother Thetis, which made him invincible: except at the heel, which was what she was holding onto as she dunked him. And so he was eventually killed by an arrow in the heel, loosed by Paris, prince of Troy, with the god Apollo's help.

Platonic

As in, "Susie's relationship with David is purely platonic, you realize."

The sort of admiring, passionate, but asexual regard for young men that Socrates engaged in. Alcibiades slept one night under a cloak with Socrates, according to Plato—but, he said, it was just like sleeping with a brother or a father. Socrates just wasn't interested in going all the way. You could see this as a metaphor for his pursuit of knowledge: it's about the quest, not the consummation.

Cynical

As in, "I'm fed up with you lot being cynical grouches. Let's bring in a bit of joy, people!"

A philosophical school, or, more accurately, way of life, practiced from the fourth century. Diogenes, who supposedly lived in a barrel, was the most famous Cynic—the word probably derives from the Greek for dog, so cynicism means "doggishness." Cynics' writings have been lost, but it seems that adherents tried to live in accordance, as much as possible, with nature, seeing animals as exemplars of anxiety-free living, and eschewing ambition, power, material possessions, even education.

Diogenes lived so in accordance with nature that he once famously masturbated in the street. Our word "cynical" thus takes a bit of leap from its ancient origins.

Stoical

As in, "Martha has been tremendously stoical since her house burned down and she lost her job."

Stoicism, founded in the fourth century by Zeno of Citium, was an extremely significant philosophical school. Empiricism and materialism were key features; in the realm of ethics, freeing oneself from emotion and living in accordance with human nature (which for Stoics is indivisible from human reason) was of great importance. Virtue, argue Stoics, was sufficient for happiness.

Skeptical

As in, "Eric claims he's going to have the dissertation ready by Thursday, but frankly, I'm skeptical."

"Skeptic" was a label introduced in the first century BC to describe the position of philosophers who held no doctrine and suspended judgement on, well, everything. Particularly lively debates ensued with the materialist Stoics. A branch of Skepticism grew from the philosophical school set up by Plato. (Called the Academy, this school was based in a gymnasium sacred to the hero Academus, whence our words academic and "the academy," meaning higher education in general.)

Epicurean

As in, "Horace, I fear you are going to have to curb your epicurean habits somewhat if you want to avoid heart problems."

Epicurus was a Samian thinker who founded a philosophical school in Athens in the late fourth century, called the Garden. Epicureans held that the phenomena of the physical world are explicable through natural causes; that man can expect no afterlife; and that the gods exist but don't involve themselves in mortals' lives. Life, then, is best devoted to pleasure—not quite the hedonism of foie gras and champagne, though; rather the removal of anxiety and the discouragement of desires that, if unsatisfied, might lead to pain. Thus the hedonism of the Epicureans in actual fact bordered on asceticism.

Arcadian

As in, "Your garden is an absolute idyll, Betty; positively Arcadian."

Arcadia is the particularly tough, rocky region of the central Peloponnese that is the legendary home of the goat god, Pan. Thanks to the Roman writer Virgil, who set his bucolic poems the *Eclogues* there, Arcadia in Renaissance European culture became the byword for lush pastoralism and cavorting, amorous nymphs and shepherds. *Et in Arcadia ego* is the famous *memento mori* coined in the early seventeenth century by the humanist cardinal who would later become Pope Clement IX. The phrase appears inscribed on a tomb, pored over by curious swains and nymphs, in two wonderful paintings by Poussin, one at Chatsworth in Derbyshire and one in the Louvre. It means, literally "I too [am] in Arcadia"—the "I," in Poussin's reading, meaning death. Evelyn Waugh took the phrase and used it for the title of the first part of his *Brideshead Revisited*, as he described the dreamy, idyllic past of his narrator's *éducation sentimentale* at Oxford.

Dog days

As in, "I've no energy to do anything in these dog days, except lie in the garden."

The dog star, the brightest in the heavens, is Sirius, originally a magical dog called Laelaps given by King Minos of Crete to the mythical princess of Athens, Procis. She was married to the great hunter Cephalus, one of the lovers of the goddess Dawn.

In the heavens, Sirius is the dog belonging to Orion, the great hunter, who is associated with Cephalus. Sirius appears at the height of summer, the dog days, presaging disease and pestilence. In the *Iliad*, when Achilles pursues Hector around the walls of Troy before slaughtering him, his flashing armor seen far off on the plain is likened to the dog star—deadly.

Golden age

As in, "Now, when good Queen Bess was on the throne, and we Brits saw off the Armada—that's what I call a golden age."

The golden age (and with it the idea of decline from some blissfully prelapsarian state) is one of the most persistent ideas in Western culture. It originally appears in Hesiod's *Works and Days*. The poet writes that the first mortals on earth, in the time of the old gods Cronus and Rhea, were perfectly happy, unafflicted by illness. The earth produced plenty for them of its own accord: they were a race made of gold. Later, a second race of silver replaced them, much inferior, who refused to sacrifice to the gods. These, in due course, were replaced by the violent, warlike bronze people. A fourth race followed: the race of heroes: this was the age of the quest for the Golden Fleece and the Trojan War. Finally came our age, the age of iron, full of toil and misery.

Olympic Games

As in, "We're constantly being told what a marvelous thing for London the Olympics are. Let's hope they don't make an almighty mess of it."

One of the few pan-Hellenic events, in its heyday drawing competitors from all over the Greek world, the Olympic Games began in 776, and kept going right up to the fourth century AD. They were founded to commemorate the victory by Pelops over King Oenomaus in a chariot race. Pelops (the fellow with the ivory shoulder, see entry under "tantalizing") used a team of winged horses, which seems rather an unfair advantage; and he also loosened the wheel on Oenomaus' chariot, so that it crashed and he died. A cynic might point out, then, that the Olympics started as they have continued: with a great deal of poor sportsmanship. Like the modern Olympics, the games took place every four years. Events included the sprint, pentathlon, wrestling, horse races, chariot races and a race in full hoplite armor. No records survive of a synchronized swimming event.

THE TEN ESSENTIAL GREEK QUOTES

Meden agan—nothing in excess.
A phrase said to have been inscribed at the temple of Apollo at Delphi. The idea is, perhaps, not to draw attention to yourself by excessively flaunting power, good fortune, etc. Herodotus' *Histories* have something of the spirit of *meden agan*: in his worldview the overmighty tend to fall. Take Xerxes, who whips the waters of the Hellespont in rage; or Croesus of Lydia, who believes himself the most fortunate man alive, only to have his empire stripped from him by the Persians.

Nowadays, commonly (though oddly) used when the speaker wishes to excuse a certain consumption of cream, cigarettes, booze, etc. For example (from a *Guardian* interview with model Jasmine Guinness): "I drink and I smoke, but not very much of either, I believe in the Greek theory of moderation, a little bit of everything is good for you."

Gnothi seauton—know yourself.
Also inscribed at the temple of Apollo in Delphi; a suitable warning/challenge, perhaps, before the visitor sallies forth into the inner sanctum and consults the oracle of the god. Latinized as *tecum nosce*, it appears in the film *The Matrix*, written above the door of the Oracle's kitchen.

Pathei mathos—wisdom comes through suffering.

The most marvelously pithy quote from the start of Aeschylus' *Agamemnon*, the first play in the *Oresteia* trilogy. Some have taken the (perhaps rather simplistic) view that *pathei mathos* sums up the progress of the whole *Oresteia*, enlightenment gradually emerging from the murky depths of bloodlust. What is certainly right is that *pathei mathos* is one of those quotes that becomes more meaningful the older you get. Useful for muttering under your breath when bad things happen.

Ktema es aei—a possession for ever.

From Thucydides' *History of the Peloponnesian War*. He's saying that his book is not meant to entertain, but will be a work of permanent value (unlike, if you read between the lines, the childish, romance-infused work of Herodotus). I find it very useful when justifying expensive purchases: "Of course it's worth having the Ofili print/1950s cocktail dress/huge book on Wyndham Lewis. It's a *ktema es aei*."

Polla ta deina—literally, many are the marvels.

This quote is the beginning of the famous chorus in Sophocles' *Antigone* about man's resourcefulness and inventiveness (see chapter 2). Extremely useful for expressing slightly dismissive or ironic surprise; the Greek version of "wonders will never cease." As in, "Eric actually did the washing up—*polla ta deina*!"

The unexamined life is not worth living—Socrates, in Plato's *Apology*. Self-explanatory.

Crito, we owe a cock to Asclepius; please pay it and don't forget it—Socrates, in Plato's *Apology*.

These were Socrates' last words, and frankly, more famous for the "say what?" factor than for anything else. No one's been able to work out quite what he meant. A cock would be sacrificed to the god of healing as a thanks offering; or to ask him to help restore someone to health. Earlier in the dialogue it was noted that Plato was ill—so it could refer to him, though it still seems a little odd. Possibly Socrates was implying that death is the cure for life.

Call no man happy until he is dead—Solon, as quoted in Herodotus' *Histories*.
It doesn't mean that only the dead are happy; rather it expresses the notion that anything can happen; you just don't know what's around the corner. It comes up when Croesus of Lydia encourages the Greek lawmaker Solon to tell him he's the most fortunate man in the world. Solon gives him to understand that you can't judge these things until you can review their entire life—fair enough, since Croesus was soon to lose his empire to the Persians. Compare the end of Sophocles' *Oedipus the King*, which expresses the same sentiment.

I would rather stand three times in the battle line than give birth once—Medea, in Euripides' *Medea*
Too right, sister. However, this sister kills her children later in the play, so perhaps we shouldn't entirely trust her proto-feminist pronouncements.

Famous men have the whole earth as their memorial—Pericles, in Thucydides' *History of the Peloponnesian War*.
It's the tear-jerky bit in Pericles' famous funeral oration about the Athenian war dead, a translation of which is inscribed on the war memorial in Edinburgh and had a powerful emotional effect on the youthful Gordon Brown (see chapter 5).

THE GREEK ALPHABET

Traditional English transliteration		Lower case	Upper case
a	Alpha	α	Α
b	Beta	β	Β
g	Gamma	γ	Γ
d	Delta	δ	Δ
e	Epsilon	ε	Ε
z	Zeta	ζ	Ζ
e	Eta	η	Η
th	Theta	θ	Θ
i	Iota	ι	Ι
k	Kappa	κ	Κ
l	Lambda	λ	Λ
m	Mu	μ	Μ
n	Nu	ν	Ν
ks	Xi	ξ	Ξ
o	Omicron	ο	Ο
p	Pi	π	Π
r	Rho	ρ	Ρ
s	Sigma	σ	Σ
t	Tau	τ	Τ
u	Upsilon	υ	Υ
f	Phi	φ	Φ
ch	Chi	χ	Χ
ps	Psi	ψ	Ψ
o	Omega	ω	Ω

FURTHER READING

These further reading suggestions reflect some of the books that I read while writing *It's All Greek To Me*, many of which I drew on very deeply, and all of which I highly recommend.

General

The Oxford Classical Dictionary, edited by Simon Hornblower and Antony Spawforth (New York, Oxford University Press, third edition, revised, 2003), is the first port of call for concise and clear guidance on individual subjects. *Ancient Greek Literature*, by Tim Whitmarsh (Malden, MA, Polity Press, 2004), is an exciting, penetrating introduction to the subject. *Classics: A Very Short Introduction*, by Mary Beard and John Henderson (New York, Oxford University Press, 1995), is a pithy, challenging way into what classics is all about. *Fifty Key Classical Authors*, by Alison Sharrock and Rhiannon Ash (New York, Routledge, 2002), contains concise articles on individual writers, and suggestions for further reading. *The Oxford Book of Classical Verse in Translation*, edited by Adrian Poole and Jeremy Maule (New York, Oxford University Press, 1995), has a great selection of Greek poetry and drama translated by poets from Hardy to Housman. Virginia Woolf's wonderful piece "On Not Knowing Greek," first published in 1925, is available in modern paperback edition—*The Common Reader Volume One* (New York, Harcourt, 1984)—along with other classic essays on writers such as George Eliot. *The Cambridge Illustrated History of Ancient Greece*, edited by Paul Cartledge (New York, Cambridge University Press, revised edition 2002), is the perfect overview of Greek history and culture; great pictures, too. *The Short Oxford History of Europe: Classical Greece*, edited by Robin Osborne (New York, Oxford University Press, 2000), is another excellent historical overview with essays by topnotch contributors.

Homer and The living, the dead, and the deathless

My favorite Homer translations are by Robert Fagles: the *Iliad* (New York, Penguin, 1998) and the *Odyssey* (New York, Penguin, 1997). Both have excellent introductions by Bernard Knox. The wonderful 1611 George Chapman translation of the *Iliad* is available in paperback (Ware, Wordsworth Editions, 2000), with an interesting introduction by Jan Parker. *The Cambridge Companion to Homer*, edited by Robert Fowler (New York, Cambridge University Press, 2004), is full of useful essays. I recommend the interview given by Stanley Lombardo, a poet-classicist who has made fine translations of Homer, to the poetry magazine *Jacket* (http://jacketmagazine.com/21/leddy-lomb-iv.html). *Homer on Life and Death* (New York, Oxford University Press, 1983), by Jasper Griffin, is a classic. Hesiod's *Theogony* and *Works and Days* are translated by M. L. West (New York, Oxford University Press, revised edition, 2008). Sophocles' *Antigone*, *Oedipus the King*, and *Oedipus at Colonus* are translated by Robert Fagles as *The Three Theban Plays* (New York, Penguin, 1984). Bernard Knox contributes excellent introductions.

Man is a political animal

For Herodotus and Thucydides see above.

If you are interested in life in ancient Athens, you must read the rich and beautifully written *Courtesans and Fishcakes*, by James Davidson (New York, St. Martin's Press, 1998). Useful are the relevant chapters in *The Cambridge Illustrated History of Ancient Greece* and *The Short Oxford History of Europe: Classical Greece* (see above). Aeschylus's *Oresteia* is translated by Richmond Lattimore (Chicago, University of Chicago Press, 1954). Aristotle's *An Inquiry Concerning Animals* is available in three volumes in the Loeb edition (parallel Greek and English text) as *Historia Animalium* (Cambridge, Harvard University Press, 1965, 1970, 1991). The essential armchair or field guide to the Parthenon is *The Parthenon*, by Mary Beard (Cambridge, Harvard University Press, 2003). Tim Whitmarsh's *Ancient Greek Literature* (see above) is, once again, very useful.

Pandora's daughters

For a translation of Aeschylus's *Oresteia*, see above. *The Bacchae* is translated by Philip Vellacott in *The Bacchae and Other Plays* (New York, Penguin, 1963).

Medea is translated by Philip Vellacott in *Medea/Hecabe/Electra/Heracles* (New York, Penguin, 1963). *Antigone* is translated as part of *The Three Theban Plays* (see above; also see above for translations of Homer, Herodotus, and Thucydides). The hilarious *The Authoress of the Odyssey*, by Samuel Butler, is available with an excellent introduction by Tim Whitmarsh (Bristol, Bristol Phoenix, 2003). For the poems of Sappho, I heartily recommend Stanley Lombardo's translation, *Sappho: Poems and Fragments* (Indianapolis, Hackett Publishing Company, 2002), with a very interesting introduction by Pamela Gordon. Gender studies is a huge and growing area in classical scholarship. Cartledge's *The Greeks: A Portrait of Self and Others* (New York, Oxford University Press, revised edition, 2002) is a good place to start. Also try *Women in the Classical World*, edited by Elaine Fantham et al (New York, Oxford University Press, 1994). James Davidson's *Courtesans and Fishcakes* (see above) is indispensable. For Spartan women, see *The Spartans: An Epic History*, by Paul Cartledge (London, Pan, 2003).

Swords and sandals
For Homer, see above.

Herodotus: The Histories are translated by Robin Waterfield (New York, Oxford University Press, 2008). I particularly recommend the notes and introduction by Caroline Dewald—some marvelous outbursts of Herodotean wit and anecdote. Thucydides' *The History of the Peloponnesian War* is translated by Rex Warner (New York, Penguin, revised edition 1972). Euripides' *The Trojan Women* is translated in *The Bacchae and Other Plays* (see above). *Persian Fire*, by Tom Holland (London, Abacus, 2006), is a racy, spirited narrative account of the Persian Wars. *The Spartans: An Epic History*, (see above), is a gripping read by one of the great ancient historians of his generation.

Beyond the borders
For Homer and Herodotus, see above.

The Greeks: A Portrait of Self and Others, by Paul Cartledge (see above), is indispensable. *Inventing the Barbarian*, by Edith Hall (New York, Oxford University Press, 1989), is an extremely influential look at how the Greeks, with particular reference to Aeschylus' play *The Persians*, saw foreigners. Tim Whitmarsh's *Ancient Greek Literature* (see above) is very useful here.

The twilight of the gods
The great works on Greek science are by the distinguished scholar G. E. R. Lloyd, especially *Early Greek Science: Thales to Aristotle*

(New York, Norton, 1971). My chapter draws deeply on it. Lloyd's *The Revolutions of Wisdom* (Berkeley, University of California Press, 1987) is a classic. Lloyd also wrote the introduction to the diverting paperback selection of translated *Hippocratic Writings* (New York, Penguin, 1983). For Aristotle's *Inquiry Concerning Animals*, see above. *Aristotle: A Very Short Introduction*, by Jonathan Barnes, is a brilliant way into the philosopher (New York, Oxford University Press, 2000). Barnes also edited *The Cambridge Companion to Aristotle* (New York, Cambridge University Press, 1995); and his work *The Pre-Socratic Philosophers* is a classic (New York, Routledge, 1999). Vivian Nutton's *Ancient Medicine* (New York, Routledge, 2004) is very useful.

The death of Socrates and the birth of philosophy

Plato's *Republic* is translated by Robin Waterfield (New York, Oxford University Press, 2008). *The Last Days of Socrates*, translated by Hugh Tredennick and Harold Tarrant (New York, Penguin, 2003), collects the dialogues relating to Socrates' death, including *Phaedo* and *Apology*. *An Introduction to Plato's Republic*, by Julia Annas (New York, Oxford University Press, 1981) is the place to start with *Republic*. It is a classic: admirably clear, beautifully written, and often very funny. Her *Plato: A Very Short Introduction* (New York, Oxford University Press, 2003) is a stimulating way into Plato generally. *Plato's Republic: A Biography*, by Simon Blackburn (New York, Atlantic Monthly Press, 2007), looks at Plato's afterlife, as does *Plato's Progeny: How Plato and Socrates Still Captivate the Modern Mind*, by Melissa Lane (London, Duckworth, 2001). *The Death of Socrates: Hero Villain, Chatterbox, Saint*, by Emily Wilson (Cambridge, Harvard University Press, 2007), is a thoroughly enjoyable, incisive look at why the Athenians killed Socrates. My section on Socrates' death draws deeply on this work.

Love and loss

For translations of Homer and Sappho, see above. *The Symposium* is translated by Robin Waterfield (New York, Oxford University Press, 1994). Page duBois's *Sappho Is Burning* (Chicago, University of Chicago Press, 1995) provides absorbing readings of the poems and fragments. An essential work is *The Greeks and Greek Love: A Bold New Exploration of the Ancient World*, by James Davidson (New York, Random House, 2009)—a startling, energizing, and consuming book.

Acknowledgments

To all at Short Books: Aurea Carpenter, Emily Fox, Rebecca Nicolson, and Vanessa Webb. To Rakesh Satyal, Rob Crawford, and the team at HarperCollins.

To Peter Straus and George Lucas.

Gratefully, to Alan Rusbridger and Nick Hopkins at the *Guardian*, for allowing me a leave of absence.

To my parents, Peter and Pamela Higgins, to whom this book is lovingly dedicated.

To the people who taught me about Greece: Cynthia Smart, Jasper Griffin, Oswyn Murray, James Davidson, the late Oliver Lyne, the late Michael Comber. And to my old comrades-in-classics, especially Antonia Potter, Joshua St. Johnston, Emily Wilson, Nick Delfas, and Emma Christian.

To the many friends who have cheered me on, including Jacqueline Riding, for living with it, and Margaret Owen, for a desk.

To Rupert Higgins and Dawn Lawrence, for ideas on Aristotle, halcyons, and giant ants.

Humbly and profoundly, to those who read and made invaluable comments on the book at various stages of its development: Professor Paul Cartledge, Dr. James Davidson, Professor Matthew Fox, Susanna Eastburn, Joshua St. Johnston, Catherine Whitaker, Dr. Tim Whitmarsh.

Above all, to Matthew, whose love, encouragement, and dry martinis make anything seem possible, and in whose inspirational company most of this book was written. *Su de moi thaleros parakoites.*

The mistakes are all my own.

Index